The Practice of Hongik Ingan

"To live for the benefit of all mankind"

Lives of Queen Seondeok, King Sejong, Saimdang and Yulgok

Published by

Diamond Sutra Recitation Group

Publisher Jae-woong Kim

Editorial Board Hyang-jin Jung, Ji-seon Lee, Hang-jin Chang,

Yoon-sang Han, Matthew Jackson

Printed and bound by Samjung Munhwasa

Chungjeong-ro 37-18, Seodaemun-gu, Seoul

The following copyrighted photographs appear with permission:

p. 20, Gyeongju National Museum;

p. 40, 68, Korea Tourism Organization;

pp. 72, 96, Ojukheon and Gangneung Municipal Museum;

pp. 88, 89, 90, 91, National Museum of Korea.

ISBN: 978-0-9797263-8-5

First edition, March 2011

Second edition, March 2013

Printed in the Republic of Korea

Note on Romanization

The Romanization of Korean words in this book follows the McCune-Reichauer

system, but omits the diacritical marks indicating vowels shifts and aspirations.

Contents

Preface

This seventh book of the Korean Spirit and Culture Series introduces four famous historical figures of Korea; Queen Seondeok (r. 632~647), King Sejong (1397~1450), Shin Saimdang (1504~1551), and Yi Yulgok (1536~1584). Queen Seondeok was the first female monarch in Korean history and laid the foundation for the unification of the Three Kingdoms of Korea (Koguryo, Paekche and Silla). King Sejong is the inventor of Korean alphabet Hangul, and Korea enjoyed a golden age under his reign. Shin Saimdang was an exceptional artist and calligraphist of the early 16th century, and for over 500 years has been held up as a model of the Confucian ideal of a devoted daughter, good wife and wise mother. Her son, Yi Yulgok, was not only a renowned scholar but also a revered politician and reformer.

The social and cultural backgrounds of these four figures differ strikingly. During the Three Kingdoms period, when Queen Seondeok was alive, Korea was deeply influenced by Buddhism as well as Taoism, and the status of women was higher than in other eras. There were three female rulers during the Silla period, and sons and daughters inherited property from their parents in equal measure. When the Choson Dynasty was founded in the 14th century, Korea's official belief system changed to Neo-Confucianism. As a result, Buddhism was suppressed, and the treatment of women worsened considerably.

While the social and philosophical climate may have changed, and in spite of differences in social position and status, at a deeper level we find the same core values in the lives of Queen Seondeok, King Sejong, Saimdang and Yulgok, who were all distinguished by their self-discipline, reverence, compassion and whole-hearted devotion. When facing great hardships, they never abandoned what they felt to be their duty, and as a result made invaluable contributions to their country and society, which remained as long-lasting legacies in the lives and the thoughts of their contemporaries and descendants. Their lives could be seen as a manifestation of *Hongik Ingan* ("To live for the benefit of all mankind"), the original founding philosophy of Korea. Viewed in this light, they transcend the boundaries of ideology and religion.

Timeline of Korean History

BC 2333~BC 108	Old Choson Dynasty: The First Kingdom of Korea (Bronze Age & Iron Age)
BC 57~AD 668	Three Kingdoms Period: Koguryo, Paekche and Silla
668	Three Kingdoms unified under Silla
668~ 935	Unified Silla
918~1392	Koryo Dynasty
1392~ 1910	Choson Dynasty
1910~1945	Japanese Occupation
1948	Korea divided into North (DPRK) and South (ROK)
1950~1953	Korean War
1988	South Korea hosts Summer Olympic Games in Seoul
1995	South Korea joins OECD
2002	South Korea and Japan Co-host 2002 FIFA World Cup
2010	South Korea hosts G20 Summit in Seoul

The first kingdom of Korea was called Choson ("Land of Morning Calm"), now often referred to as "Old Choson" to distinguish it from the later dynasty of the same name founded in the 14th century. Old Choson was founded by Tangun Wanggum in 2333 BC, on the principle of *Hongik Ingan*, which means "to live and work for the benefit of all mankind." While various religions including Buddhism, Taoism, Confucianism and Christianity have had a great influence on Korea over different periods of history, the teaching of *Hongik Ingan* has endured through the ages as the spiritual foundation of the Korean people.

Queen Seondeok: Korea's First Female Leader

1,400 years ago in Korea, in the kingdom of Silla, King Chinpyong was concerned that he had no son to whom he could give the crown. Recognizing the achievements of his first royal son-in-law, Yongchun, as a leader in the elite youth forces or *Hwarang*, he decided to abdicate the throne in his favor.

Aware of his intention, the second princess, Tokman, went to the king and said, "Father, I request that you make Yongchun my subject."

The king was surprised, for it was clear that his daughter was asking for the throne. He was so impressed by her spirit, however, that he eventually succeeded in having princess Tokman appointed as the new heir to the throne.

The king regretted that she had not been born a man, but considering the remarkable courage of the princess, he had faith in her potential to become a great leader. In deference to her request, he commanded his son-in-law Yongchun to pledge his allegiance to the new Queen.

So it was that Queen Seondeok came to power as the 27th ruler of the Silla kingdom, and the first female monarch in Korean history.

1. Silla: the Unifier of Korea, and its Smallest Kingdom

For a full understanding of the political situation in Silla during this period, a brief summary of the history of the Three Kingdoms of Korea is needed first.

In the first century B.C., three rival kingdoms, Koguryo, Paekche and Silla, were established as separate nations in the Korean peninsula. Koguryo was located in the North; most of its territory was mountainous, and therefore unsuitable for agriculture. In such circumstances, Koguryo successfully defended herself against the continually invading forces of China, and steadily built up her power against the influence of her formidable neighbor.

Koguryo had recovered the states of Yodong and Manchuria from China. These states had originally been part of Korea during the Old Choson period (2333-108 B.C.), and thus expanded Korea's territory to the largest extent in the country's history. Koguryo was at its zenith during the 5th century, when it gained supremacy in the home peninsula and went on to become the strongest power in East Asia.

The kingdom of Paekche lay in the southwest of the peninsula, covering the present day provinces of Chungchong and Cholla. It was blessed with the largest fertile area of agricultural land among the three kingdoms, and so enjoyed the greatest economic prosperity. Fully exploiting its geographical advantages, it became a focal point of ancient commerce, serving as a trading intermediary between China and Japan.

The kingdom of Silla was slowest to develop, with strong tribal traditions hindering its progress as a unified state. Being in the mountainous southeast, it further suffered from a scarcity of farmland. From the 6th century B.C. however, under the reign of King Chinhung, Silla greatly increased and expanded its influence and power. By capturing the basin of the Han River, previously held by Paekche, it came to occupy the most strategically valuable point in the whole peninsula, and was in a position to threaten even Koguryo in the north.

In the early 7th century, during the reign of Queen Seondeok, the first foundations for a unified Korea under Silla were laid. A series of attacks by Paekche had brought the kingdom to a point of crisis, and the Queen made the decision to form an alliance with the Chinese Tang Dynasty. Not long afterwards, in 660 A.D., the Silla-Tang coalition was victorious over the forces of Paekche and conquered the entire kingdom, under the command of the new Silla King Muyol (Kim Chun-chu) and his general, Kim Yusin. The process of unification was completed eight years later when Koguryo finally admitted defeat before the forces of the alliance.

From that time onward, Tang China began to make its influence felt in the former territories of Koguryo and Paekche, and eventually came to threaten Silla itself. In 670 A.D., war broke out between the two powers, when Silla crossed the Amnok River to attack its former ally.

Victory in two critical battles at Maesosong (675) and Kibolpo (676) enabled Silla eventually to drive out the Tang from the peninsula, and thus the integration of the three kingdoms was completed. The separate states of Korea were, for the first time, established together as one nation, known from then on as Unified Silla.

How was it possible for a small and remote country to defeat the kingdoms of Paekche and Koguryo, overcome the formidable Tang forces, and bring the country under one rule? Behind the means which accomplished this great task, there lay the sincere and cherished resolve of a single mind. It was Queen Seondeok's earnest devotion that moved and guided the Silla people, and the concentrated power of her will which enabled the dream of a unified Korea to become a reality.

2. A Princess Worthy to be Queen

Queen Seondeok served as monarch for 16 years, from 632 to 647. Her family name was Kim, and her given name Tokman. In the famous historical work of ancient Korea, *Samguksagi* (History of the Three Kingdoms), her character is described as "generous, benevolent, ingenious, and insightful."

Queen Seondeok was first to break the tradition that only a man could lead the country, thus challenging a common preconception of the day. However, the fact that she was able to do so in the first place implies that the women of her country enjoyed a higher status than was normal in the East at that time. This was indeed the case. In Silla, daughters and sons inherited on equal terms, and women were free to remarry if they chose. In *Sintangso* (Revised History of the Tang Dynasty), it is related in the Silla Chapter, "Women are doing all the buying and selling in the marketplace nowadays." We can infer from this that women actively participated in social and economic activities. We learn also that certain female figures in the history of Silla, such as the Holy Mother of Mt. Sondo, and the wives of Park Hyokgose and Park Chesang, were revered as national goddesses, and that there was a long-standing tradition in Silla that priestly orders be made open to women as well as men. All this evidence gives us a clear impression of the status women enjoyed in the Silla of Queen Seondeok's day.

Despite such favorable circumstances, princess Tokman's path to the throne was beset with difficulty. In 631, a year before her coronation, two government officials, Chilsuk and Sokpum, rose up in revolt against her succession. In spite of opposition and resistance, both from within her kingdom and abroad, Tokman was able to take the crown, for she was indeed worthy to rule as Queen. The support of a strong king, her father Chinpyong goes some way to explaining her success, but it is not enough. By asking her father for the throne, it was Seondeok who took the initiative in setting aside the tradition that a woman could not act as ruler. To prepare for her role at the head of her country, she took care to develop her personal abilities, in particular good judgment and integrity.

3. The Political Power of Queen Seondeok

In the beleaguered years of the mid-7th century, with repeated invasions by the forces of Paekche and Koguryo, a rebellion led by State Secretary Pidam against her royal authority towards the end of her reign, and the all-powerful Chinese Emperor Taizong openly scorning her unmarried status, Queen Seondeok was nevertheless responsible for many splendid achievements, thanks to her profound wisdom and political ability.

Her first concern as ruler was the livelihood of the people. Directly after her coronation, she sent royal inspectors to every province to oversee the care and maintenance of widows, widowers, orphans, poor and elderly who had no family to support them. Through this act of kindness, the Queen won the people's support, and her position was strengthened against opposition from the male aristocracy.

This accomplished, she began to promote friendly relations with China, sending representatives and paying tribute in the December after her enthronement and in July the following year. This attempt to secure the goodwill of China was a diplomatic ploy to discourage military incursions from Paekche and Koguryo. Emperor Taizong, however, openly despised the Queen's overtures and humiliated her envoys with insults.

In September 643, the twelfth year of her reign, Silla requested reinforcements from China to deter repeated offensives from the Paekche-Koguryo coalition. Emperor Taizong refused the petition, with the reply, "Ever since your country gave the royal crown to a mere woman, your neighbors have held you in contempt. You are like a country which has lost its king and freely welcomed in the ranks of the enemy. It is therefore small wonder that you are unable to enjoy peace for a single year." He further declared, "We have decided that a member of our own royal house will act as the new king of Silla. Naturally he will need an army to support him, and so I will have my troops protect your country for the present time, and allow you to govern yourselves when peace is restored." This message from the Emperor caused great alarm, for it was clearly his intention to turn Silla into a vassal state of China. Queen Seondeok, however, did not openly oppose Chinese intervention, but chose a more prudent course. In the January of the following year, she dispatched an envoy to the emperor with a selection of her country's finest delicacies and other luxurious items in order to appease him. Sure enough, the plans for intervention were later dropped.

Queen Seondeok's father King Chinpyong had kept up good relations with China during his reign, in order to avoid the danger of Silla becoming isolated. Queen Seondeok continued to send ambassadors and students to China, following his example. In time, China realized that Silla could be of great use to them as a check on their powerful enemy Koguryo, and eventually decided to recognize Queen Seondeok officially as King Chinpyong's successor to the throne.

For Silla, the maintenance of friendly diplomatic relations with China was an unavoidable necessity. For the sake of the kingdom's survival and security, the Queen had no choice but to accept every humiliation offered. This dogged policy of endurance prepared the way for a lasting friendship with China, and so it was in large part thanks to her efforts that King Muyol was later able to enjoy harmonious relations with China, and the campaign to bring the three kingdoms together could be undertaken with its assistance. If Korea's unification were compared to a fall harvest, Queen Seondeok was the farmer who endured the burning sun and heavy rains of the summer.

4. Seondeok's Skillful Use of Government Posts

As a female ruler in a society dominated by males, Queen Seondeok overcame her disadvantage by making the best use she could of the men in her court. The most striking examples are those of Kim Chun-chu and Kim Yusin, who were in charge of general political affairs.

Kim Chun-chu was the grandson of King Chinji. Chinji had been dethroned for misgovernment by the nobles. He was also the son of Kim Yongchun, who had originally competed with Seondeok for the crown. He could therefore have become one of her most bitter adversaries. Rather than alienating him by branding him as a potential rebel, Queen Seondeok eventually succeeded in making him her most loyal subject. By entrusting him with foreign affairs, she gave him a chance to make full use of his abilities. Kim Chun-chu never challenged the Queen's position; on the contrary, he remained her steadfast supporter throughout his long and distinguished service.

The case of Kim Yusin, now one of Korea's greatest national heroes thanks to his role in unifying the country, also shows us her wisdom in dealing with men. Kim Yusin had originally been a member of the royal house of the Kaya Kingdom, which had been destroyed by Silla in the 6th century. Although the royal family of Kaya were admitted into the *Chin-gol* class of the Silla nobility (then second to the *Song-gol* class, whose members alone were eligible for the throne), the aristocracy were never fully able to accept them. He was thus a nobleman in name alone, and in reality a foreigner who suffered from discrimination. Queen Seondeok recognized his potential as a leader, and helped to strengthen his position by arranging a marriage between his sister and Kim Chun-chu, who later became king. Though there is no doubt that ability and diligent effort were the basis of his achievements, Silla was nonetheless a class-conscious society where even the most outstanding personal abilities could be held in check by social status. It is reasonable to say that he could never have become established in a public career without the support of the Queen.

5. Alliance between Kim Chun-chu and Kim Yusin

There is an interesting story about the family alliance between Kim Chun-chu and Kim Yusin. Yusin had two sisters called Pohee and Munhee. Pohee was of shy disposition and delicate appearance, while Munhee was a tall and outgoing girl.

One morning, Pohee awoke to find herself blushing. When Munhee questioned her about it, she confessed that she had had a strange dream the night before. In the dream, Pohee had urinated until the capital city was underwater. Realizing that this was no ordinary dream, Munhee gave Pohee a silk dress, and bought the dream from her.

A few days later, Chun-chu came to Yusin's house for a game of *Kyokgu* (a sport played on horseback). During the game, Yusin accidentally tore off one of the tassels on Chun-chu's robe. Yusin sent for Pohee to mend the garment, but she was too nervous to come into the presence of a stranger. Munhee therefore came out to mend the tie instead of Pohee, and when they met, Chun-chu and Munhee fell in love with one another. Yusin hoped that the two would marry, but Chun-chu hesitated to propose to Munhee since he already had a wife. In the meantime, Munhee fell pregnant. Yusin scolded her severely for becoming pregnant out of wedlock, and declared in public that he would have her burned alive in punishment.

Not long afterwards, Queen Seondeok was walking with her officials on the Namsan Mountain. Hearing about this, Yusin made a pile of dry logs and twigs in the garden outside his house, and set it alight. High up on the mountain, the Queen was able to make out the black clouds of smoke, and asked those accompanying her if they knew the reason. None dared to answer her, but simply looked at one another in embarrassment. When the Queen pressed the issue, she finally learned from them that Yusin was on the point of burning his sister and her unborn child at the stake.

She was astonished, and exclaimed, "It is not in his character to do such a thing! There must be a reason. Who could the father be?" Chun-chu, who was present, blushed scarlet and was speechless with embarrassment. After the truth was revealed, the Queen ordered him to go and save Munhee's life, granting him permission to marry her as his second wife, and for her to become his lawful spouse when his first wife passed away. When Chun-chu later came to the throne as King Muyol, the 29th ruler of Silla after Seondeok and her sister Chindok, Munhee thus became his queen. Their child grew up to be King Mun-mu, who completed the unification of Korea twenty nine years after Queen Seondeok's death.

In fact, the tearing of Chun-chu's robe and his publicly-announced intention to kill his sister Munhee were part of an elaborate plan. Thanks to the Queen's royal favor, Yusin and Chun-chu were able to form kinship through marriage. And through this tie of kinship, a political alliance was formed which swiftly brought the process of unification to its fulfillment.

6. The Nine-story Pagoda at Hwang Ryong Sa Temple

In 642, eleven years after Queen Seondeok had come to power, persistent enemy invasions had resulted in forty castles in the western part of Silla falling to Paekche. The enemy, who had now combined forces with Koguryo, were now close to taking Tang-hang Castle, a fort which bridged Silla and China, and which was therefore a position of great importance to Silla. The country was helpless in the face of this disaster, and not far from total ruin. At this point of crisis, Queen Seondeok sent for the renowned Buddhist monk Chajang, who was studying abroad at the time.

Chajang returned to Silla in 643, having been abroad for seven years. Standing before the Queen and her counselors, he proposed the building of a great nine-story pagoda, with the combined purpose of blocking foreign invasion and furthering the larger task of unification by uniting the minds of the people.

Although the Queen was pleased with his proposal, she could not accept it without hesitation. The new construction project would place a heavy burden of tax and labor on her subjects, who were already weary from incessant warfare. After careful reflection, she decided to proceed, seeing it as a task of national importance necessary to overcome the present danger and eventually to unify the peninsula. Having come to this conclusion, she requested the opinion of her courtiers on the matter, and learned that they were strongly opposed to it, owing to the condition of the state treasury. The Queen decided to press ahead with the plan, however, in her firm belief that a work of religious devotion would bring the people together to deal with the current crisis. Those who objected on financial grounds she calmed by giving her assurance, "If we lack the means, tear down my palace and use its bricks and timbers."

After two years, the great pagoda was finally completed. Inside it, Chajang enshrined the *sarira* (holy relics of the Buddha) which he had brought from China.

Model of Hwang Ryong Sa Temple (Gyeongju National Museum)

The nine levels of the pagoda stood for the peoples of nine different countries, including Japan and various other districts which are now part of China and Korea. According to the ancient architectural record *Chiljugi*, the pagoda was 80 meters in height. This is as high as a twenty-storey apartment block today, and an almost unheard of size for a building in those days. The pagoda was a physical manifestation of the earnest wish of Queen Seondeok and the Silla people to protect the country and eventually bring the three kingdoms together. At the same time, it was an offering made to the Buddha with the utmost sincerity, in the hope that these wishes would be fulfilled.

In the year 1282, during the Mongolian invasion, the pagoda was burned to the ground, and today only the cornerstone survives. At the site of the Hwang Ryong Sa Temple, however, the spirit of Silla's magnificent cultural heritage endures, even after the passing of 1,300 years.

7. The Queen's Compassion for her People

The following story shows us the compassionate nature of Queen Seondeok. In the Silla kingdom, there lived a young carriage bearer of humble birth named Chigwi, who greatly admired the Queen in spite of their differences in age and social status.

He had first encountered Seondeok as she passed him in the street while on a visit to the capital city, and had fallen in love with her at first sight. He stopped eating and sleeping, and did nothing but call out the name of the Queen all day. Eventually, he went out of his mind.

One day soon afterwards, the Queen went to visit a Buddhist temple. As she was passing a certain street corner, Chigwi appeared, calling out the Queen's name as usual, and was immediately thrust aside by the Queen's guards. The sight greatly stirred the onlookers, who lined the whole street. When Queen

Queen Seondeok portrayed in an MBC TV Series in 2009

asked one of her attendants about the disturbance, he answered, "Your majesty, a madman who tried to approach your royal person was apprehended by the royal guard."

"Why did they prevent him from coming to see me?" the Queen asked. The attendant was ashamed, as if he himself had committed a fault, and said, "Let me inform you then, Your Majesty, that the man in question is named Chigwi, and is known to admire you."

The Queen's heart was touched, and she ordered the attendant to allow Chigwi to follow with her retinue to the temple, to the surprise of the crowd, and to the delight of Chigwi, who danced for joy.

As the Queen was praying in the temple, Chigwi waited outside, sitting at the base of a pagoda. It was a long time before she came out, and so Chigwi at first grew bored, and then impatient as time passed. Eventually, he fell asleep.

When the Queen finally appeared, her eyes were met with the curious sight of Chigwi asleep beneath the pagoda. She gazed at him thoughtfully for a while. Then, taking a gold ring off her finger, she placed it gently on his chest. After she had gone back to the palace, Chigwi awoke and was overwhelmed with joy to find the ring the Queen had left him. According to one story, as he clasped it tightly, his joy soon turned into a fire. The fierce flames of his love burned up the pagoda and Chigwi himself, until nothing remained of him but a fiery wraith.

From this tale we learn of the Queen's great beauty, which made a common man forget his position, become lovesick, and eventually die in the flames of passion. What is even clearer, however, is the noble character of the Queen, who accepted the devotion of an ordinary man, who dared to love so far above himself.

An ordinary person might have been surprised or troubled by his attention. If Seondeok had been intolerant or self-possessed, she might have had him imprisoned or even executed for slighting her dignity. Contrary to what one might expect, the Queen tried to understand the unfortunate love of her humble subject. When Chigwi fell asleep waiting for her, she could have taken offence, as it was a most indecorous thing to happen in the presence of a queen. The guards must have been for shaking the man awake, while her courtiers would have urged her to hurry back to the palace and her appointments. Queen Seondeok, however, asked for silence and waited for a moment, looking at Chigwi with gentle eyes and a calm smile. Since he continued to sleep, the Queen left him her own ring so that he would not be disappointed when he later woke up.

Her love for Chigwi was not romantic, but she chose to empathize with his feelings rather than ignore or reject them coldly. It is worth remembering that, during her reign in Silla, the kingdom was constantly at war, and she was always having to fend off invasions from neighboring kingdoms. In these circumstances, it is truly extraordinary that she was able to keep a heart so warm and loving towards her people, and the memory of this lives on to touch our hearts today.

8. A Ruler of Great Wisdom and Foresight

During her sixteen years as ruler, Queen Seondeok is said to have perceived things that were beyond the comprehension of those around her, even enabling her to foretell the future on some occasions. Three notable examples of her insight and perception are narrated here.

Emperor Taizong of China once sent the Queen a painting depicting three peony flowers – one red, one purple and one white – together with some seeds. When the Queen had the seeds planted in her garden, she predicted that the flowers would have no scent. Time proved her words to be correct; until the very moment they wilted and died, the flowers never gave out any fragrance. Her courtiers were surprised that she had known this from the beginning, and in response to their questioning she answered, "The painting showed no butterfly beside the flowers. When he sent me this gift, Taizong was mocking me because I have no husband."[1]

This anecdote demonstrates the Queen's sharp intellect and powers of observation rather than any supernatural intelligence. From the fact that bees and butterflies are known to gather around flowers, she inferred that the flowers in the painting had no scent. Emperor Taizong's implicit ridicule of Queen Seondeok's celibacy as related here also illustrates for us the refined level of intellectual competition between the two monarchs. Outdoing the emperor in taste and good grace, Queen Seondeok later responded by founding a Buddhist temple which she named Pun Hwang Sa, or the Royal Fragrance Temple.

Five years after her enthronement, the Queen caused wonder among her people by defeating an invading enemy force with the help of frogs. Near the banks of the Song-jin River in the capital city, there was a temple called Yong Myo Sa. In the temple grounds was a pond named Ok Mun, which means, literally, "Jade Gate." On a certain day in winter, a number of frogs gathered together at the pond and began to croak loudly for several days. When this strange phenomenon was reported to the Queen, she immediately ordered two of her generals to lead two thousand of her finest soldiers to the western suburb of the city, and to look for a valley named "Yo Geun Gok" (Cradle of Life). She added that an enemy force would be found lying in wait there, which they would

---

[1] Not being married was regarded as highly dubious in the social climate of the day, and regarded as a question mark over one's character. This insult was intended to be very offensive indeed.

be sure to take by surprise. The two generals led their armies to the western suburb, found the valley the Queen had mentioned, which lay near Mt. Pu, and destroyed not only the detachment of five hundred Paekche soldiers they found there, but also a force of twelve hundred reinforcements that came later to aid them.

Her bewildered subjects asked the Queen how the croaking of frogs had informed her of the Paekche invasion. The Queen explained, "A group of angry frogs signifies an army. 'Jade Gate' is an expression for a woman's chastity. Woman is one of the meanings of Yin, which also has the meaning of white, and the white color stands for the West. So, I knew that an army was lying in the West. As we say, a man is supposed in some sense to die during the act of creating new life. Since the Paekche army was hiding in the valley known as the Cradle of Life, I knew that it would be easy to defeat them." All who heard the Queen's reasoning were amazed by her insight.

In this way, Seondeok defeated the enemy without the need for a major battle. She was well-versed in the philosophy of Yin and Yang, and interpreted all the icons correctly: Female=Yin=White=West. It is remarkable also to see the Queen's reference to the symbolic "death" of the male during the process of conception. Even today, it is not usual or easy to talk about such things in public. 1,300 years ago, the Queen openly dealt with the topic in front of her male courtiers, who were most likely embarrassed by her candidness.

The third story concerns the Queen's death. One day, although in good health, she announced before her subjects that she would die on a certain day in a certain year, and requested to be buried in the *Torichon*, which in Buddhism refers to a heavenly realm. When asked where the *Torichon* was, she replied that it was on the southern side of Mt. Nang. As she had predicted, she passed away on the foretold day and year, and was duly buried on the sunny side of the Nang mountain.

Thirty-two years later, King Mun-mu founded Temple of the Four Devas on the same mountain, some way beneath the Queen's royal tomb on the slope of the Nang Mountain. According to the Theravada Buddhist scripture *Kusaron* (倶舍論), Heaven has many levels; above the Heaven of the Four Devas lies the *Torichon*, where thirty-three heavenly gods reside. Thus, when the Four Devas Temple was built below her tomb, the Queen's prophecy finally came true, and her extraordinary powers of perception were once again revealed to the people.

A famous novelist once remarked, "The day before you die, you are sure to buy a new pair of shoes." For all of us, there is nothing more certain than death, and nothing less certain than when it will come. Queen Seondeok knew when she would die and where her body would rest; furthermore, she asked to be buried in a place which did not exist on earth, and in the end her wish was granted. It is certain that the Queen's noble wish to make Silla into Buddha's realm remains with her in the tomb at *Torichon*.

9. Everlasting Fragrance of Silla

In 1429, the 17-year old heroine Joan of Arc went to war in obedience to God's voice, which told her to save France from disaster. Her incredible patriotism, loyalty and courage all stemmed from a revelation she received from God.

The Buddhist faith was to Queen Seondeok what the Christian faith was to Joan of Arc, the foundation of all her life and works. It was her religious devotion and belief that enabled her to exercise benevolent rule and make so many great accomplishments. During her reign, Silla built eighteen temples, as well as pagodas and Buddha statues that would turn out to be the finest of the age. The Queen often visited Hwang Ryong Sa temple to pray for the wisdom and strength to save Silla from danger. By dint of sheer determination, she had the Great Pagoda built there, in the face of widespread opposition, so that the people of Silla might come to realize fully that the task of unification was their own responsibility and within their own power. The temple itself is an embodiment of her devotion to Buddha, her love for her people and country, and her great vow to achieve unification, whilst remaining celibate for her entire life. The Hwang Ryong Sa temple continued to be a source of support and inspiration for her countrymen long after her death, and it is no coincidence that many of the greatest Korean Buddhist masters, including Master Wonhyo, went on to study and achieve enlightenment there.

Making her way to the throne against the claims of men, and later enduring derision at home and abroad for being an unmarried woman; devoting herself to the care of her kingdom's people, and strengthening her weak nation's influence among the other warring kingdoms of the day; relieving the oppressed and defenseless among her subjects, shrewdly avoiding dissension and mutiny among her courtiers; making friends of rivals, enemies and foreign nations by good judgment and restraint; leaving behind temples and monuments that speak of her vision and deep wisdom, no less than of her insight and skillful planning; in one life, founded upon a devotion to her country and to Buddha, we find a sacred legacy of virtue.

The scent of a flower cannot spread against the wind, but the fragrance of virtue scents the air on every side. Queen Seondeok, everlasting flower of the Silla kingdom, makes our present day fragrant with the scent of a virtue that has endured through centuries of history.

References

Historical sources

Samguk Yusa (Memorabilia of the Three Kingdoms) by Ilyon
Samguk Sagi (History of the Three Kingdoms) by Kim Pusik

Other sources

Kim, Jong-Sung. *Silla's Unification and the Culture of the Three Kingdoms*. Seoul: Munyei, 2004.
Park, Soon-Jung. *Great Wisdom Revealed Through Queen Seondeok*. Seoul: Oneul, 2000.

King Sejong: The Everlasting Light of Korea

The Chinese of the early 15th century referred to their ruler as the "Son of the Heavens". The isolationist state of Japan gave the title "Ruler of the Heavens" to its emperor. At a time when the monarchs of neighbouring states were glorifying their offices with divine-like honours, King Sejong of Korea established the notion of the "People of the Heavens." Sejong, who revered each and every one of his people as a being of Heavenly origin and served them as such, believed that it was his duty as king to look after a noble, heavenly race.

Sejong's care and attention extended to every member of his kingdom. Female servants in government office, for example, were given thirty days of leave prior to giving birth, and a further 100 days of leave afterwards. Husbands were granted thirty days of paternity leave. Sejong also considered the rights of prisoners, frequently inquiring about the temperatures at which the prisons were kept, and ensuring that they were clean and properly maintained.

The "People of the Heavens," in King Sejong's view, were not simply the people of Korea. Even foreign peoples, such as the tribes of Jurchens, then considered by Korea and China as barbarians, he believed were no less worthy of his respect and care. His views are all the more remarkable if we consider that this was an age in which men were classed as either civilized or barbaric according to common perception.

Sejong did not regard his people simply as objects of his care and governance, but believed that they possessed a boundless potential to transform, realize, and awaken themselves to a higher level of culture and spiritual development. The real duty of kings and officials, he believed, was to help the people achieve this inner goal. The considerable effort he devoted to developing the new alphabet Hangul and to making advances in printing technology for the publication of books on many different subjects, was to achieve this one goal of helping the heavenly race of mankind educate and improve itself.

"To share with Heaven's People in the joys of living" was the goal of King Sejong, and he never rested for a moment in his pursuit of it. When his people starved during times of famine, he ate no food and prepared himself for death, offering up prayers to Heaven for a good harvest. Even when his eyesight became seriously impaired and his health grew critical, he devoted himself wholly to the betterment of the country. He fortified the nation's defences by strengthening the army and improving the standard of its weaponry. He also made radical innovations in the sciences, particularly in agriculture, medicine and astronomy. A scientific dictionary, published in Japan in 1983, recorded that in the first half of the 15th century, while no scientific achievements were made in Japan, 29 were made in Korea, compared with 5 in China, and 28 in the rest of the world. In step with scientific progress, literature and the arts also flourished, and the general standard of living rose substantially.

King Sejong the Great

1. Prince Chungnyong

Sejong was born on the 15th of May, 1397 (April 10th according to the lunar calendar) and given the birth name of To. He was the third son of Queen Wonkyong and King Taejong, himself the third monarch of the Choson Dynasty (1392~1910). At the age of 12, To became a prince and was given the name of Chungnyong.

Prince Chungnyong had two elder brothers, Yangnyong and Hyoryong. Prince Yangnyong was of burly physique and lively disposition. Although he was talented in both poetry and calligraphy, he eschewed a quiet life of study behind the nine fast-closed gates of the palace, preferring adventurous pursuits in the outside world. Prince Hyoryong, on the other hand, was tender-hearted in nature, obedient to his parents and generous to his siblings. He later became a Buddhist monk and founded many temples.

In the Confucian system observed during the Choson Dynasty, it was customary for the eldest prince to succeed to the throne. Accordingly, Prince Yangnyong was proclaimed Crown Prince at the age of 11. Crown Prince Yangnyong began to take daily lessons in the classics and in royal etiquette, learning from the scholars of the court. However, much to the disappointment of King Taejong, Yangnyong soon lost all interest in study, and instead would go out shooting with his bow and arrow, or climb over the palace wall concealed in the company of his servants. He would summon wild companions to the palace to drink with him, and spend the night singing or laughing at lewd entertainments.

Yangnyong had a reputation also as a philanderer. Learning of the rumoured beauty of Ori, a concubine of Kwak Chong, vice counselor to the King's Central Council, he ordered his servants to bring her to the palace, and made her his mistress.

The King reprimanded Yangnyong whenever reports of such behavior reached his ears, and the prince was compelled to read out statements of contrition before the spirits of his ancestors in the Royal Shrine. Eventually, however, his habits of drinking and gallantry became hardened. King Taejong was so distraught at the conduct of his son, whom he found to be unworthy of the throne, that he could hardly bear to look him in the face. Other members of the court had grown deeply concerned about the abnormal behavior of the Crown Prince and worried for the future of the state.

Eventually, a co-ordinated appeal against the Crown Prince emerged. The Prime Minister, chiefs of the six cabinet ministries, the supreme military councilors, and various dignitaries from other government bodies presented a request to the throne under joint signature to depose Yangnyong as the Crown Prince, seeing that he had shown no sign of repentance for his sins, asserting that his wild behavior was inimical to the state.

King Taejong, who had long pondered the issue in private, approved the request for deposal. Accordingly, on the 2nd of June 1418, the title of Crown Prince was removed from Yangnyong, leaving the question of whom to choose as his successor.

At this time Prince Chungnyong, the youngest of the three princes, was twenty-two years old. He had read almost all the books kept in the palace library and was more knowledgeable than many great scholars of the day. His noble character and gentle behavior conformed to the ancient standards of a wise sovereign. He was universally admired and accorded the highest respect by those who knew him.

Chungnyong, later named Sejong, was therefore inaugurated as Crown Prince in June 1418 at the age of 22, taking the place of his older brother. In the August of the same year, he ascended to the throne as the Choson Dynasty's fourth monarch.

Yangnyong's erratic behaviour did not change even after his deposal, to his family's great disappointment. Nevertheless, Sejong always treated his elder brother with sincere affection, often inviting him to the palace banquets in spite of vigorous opposition from other officials. Whenever tales of Yangnyong's misconduct were reported to the court, Sejong persuaded the officials not to make them an issue. Sejong also maintained a close relationship with his other brother, Prince Hyoryong, who became a Buddhist monk, all throughout his life.

2. Sejong's Devotion to Learning

Since early childhood, Sejong had always loved to read. Once he had read a book, he would read it again a hundred times. Some books he read over two hundred times until he had learned them by heart. Seeing his son's devotion to reading and study, King Taejong grew anxious for his health and forbade him to read during the night. When his reading at night continued, Taejong sent an attendant to confiscate and hide all the books in his room. Disheartened, Sejong began to search the room, and found one book that had escaped the attendant's notice, called Kuso Sugan (Ou-Su's letters) lying behind a screen. Overcome with joy, he picked it up and proceeded to read it several hundred times. When he learned of this, his father King Taejong said, "Why subject your body to such hardships, as if you were a scholar preparing for the state examination?"

Sejong's desire to learn grew even stronger when he became king and began to attend the Kyong-yon, where he studied and discussed Confucian Classics and historical texts with the country's most accomplished scholarly officials.

After ascending to the throne in July 1418, Sejong began to hold the Kyong-yon in October, and attended it at least once a week. By the end of his reign, Sejong had participated in 1,898 of its lectures.

As time passed, various problems arose with the holding of the Kyong-yon. The officials in charge were obliged to perform their routine government duties in addition to preparing for the meeting, and as a result were often unable to do so adequately. Furthermore, the young king's knowledge was already so advanced and his zeal for literature so fervent that the quantity and depth of the instruction he required was often difficult to provide. To solve this problem, Sejong appointed full-time teachers to manage the Kyong-yon, laying the foundations of what eventually became the Chiphyonjon or Jade Hall.

3. Chiphyonjon, the Hall of Scholars

In response to Sejong's request for the establishment of a royal institute of research, the Chiphyonjon was established within the palace grounds in March 1420, the second year of his reign.

Ten scholars initially resided there, and the number later grew to twenty. The number increased again to thirty-two when a national project was being undertaken, and returned to twenty after it was completed. As we learn from the *Kukjo Pangmok*, all but one of the scholars who resided at the Chiphyonjon during the institution's existence had succeeded in the state examination, and just under half were among the top five in their year. Although joining the Chiphyonjon at a very young age, usually around 23 or 24, they were clearly a very talented group.

Sejong earnestly supported these scholars in the belief that they were essential to the country's livelihood. As residents of the Chiphyonjon, they enjoyed many privileges. Sejong ordered the stewards of the Royal Palace to take charge of their meals, providing them on occasions with the kingdom's finest food and drink. The King would often visit the Chiphyonjon in person to encourage the scholars in their studies. They were also granted exemption from routine administrative duties and the mandatory cycle of offices, as well as special leave for intensive periods of study at home or at Buddhist temples in the peace of the mountains.

Once, as the King was taking a walk in the Royal Palace late at night, he saw a lamp burning in the Chiphyonjon, where a scholar named Sin Suk-ju was reading, forgetful of sleep. Sejong returned to his room, and ordered one of his servants to observe the scholar's movements. Upon learning from the servant later that the light had not been put out until dawn, the King went to the Chiphyonjon and gently placed his konryongpo (a royal coat made of silk) over Sin Suk-ju, who was now asleep, and sometime afterwards went to bed himself. As soon as the young scholar awoke, he saw that the King's coat had been put over his body and had kept him warm all night. Astonished by this act of kindness, he bowed towards the King's chambers with tears in his eyes.[2]

Sejong took on many projects in the thirty-two years of his reign, all of which contributed to the welfare of the public but took many years to complete. He was determined to achieve perfection in these projects, and made extensive use of the intellectual resources available to him at the Chiphyonjon.

The duties assigned to the scholars ranged widely from purely academic assignments to more active advisory roles in politics. They included the preparation of lectures for the Kyong-yon, historical and cultural research, an investigative study of the rituals and institutions of ancient dynasties, administration of the state examinations, the collection of an extensive library, and publishing works of literature deemed important to the welfare of the country. Of the duties assigned to the Chiphyonjon scholars, the last was the most demanding. Eighty new books and several hundred pamphlets and reports were published through the Chiphyonjon during the reign of King Sejong, covering the topics of politics, history, literature, linguistics, geography, philosophy, law, music, agriculture, medicine, astronomy, and others.

The most noteworthy publications included Nongsa Chiksol (A Plain Guide to Farming, 1429), Taejong Sillok (The Annals of King Taejong, 1431), Paldo Chiriji (The Geographical Descriptions of the Eight Provinces, 1432), Samgang Haengsildo (Illustrated Guide to Conduct and the Three Bonds, 1432), Hyangyak Chipsongbang (Great Collection of Native Korean Prescriptions, 1433), Chachi Tonggam Hunie (Notes on the History of China, 1436), Hunmin Chongum (The Proper Sounds to Instruct the People, 1446), Tongguk Chongum (Dictionary of Proper Korean Pronunciations, 1447), and Koryosa (The History

---

[2] *Yolryosil Kisul* (Collected Works of History by Yi Kung-ik)

Kyongbokgung Palace

of Koryo, 1450).

The number and variety of books published through the Chiphyonjon demonstrates King Sejong's determination to improve the daily life of all his subjects regardless of their class or status through wise government and the study of literature. Though the Chiphyonjon existed for a relatively brief period of thirty six years, it earned an unparalleled reputation for its lasting cultural achievements, which together comprise an important legacy for the nation of Korea.

4. Hangul, Alphabet of Love

The perfect alphabet may be a hopelessly remote ideal, but it is possible to do a better job than history has made of the western alphabet, in any of its manifestations. We know this because there is an alphabet that is about as far along the road towards perfection as any alphabet is likely to get. Emerging in Korea in mid-fifteenth century, it has the status among language scholars normally reserved for classic works of art. In its simplicity, efficiency and elegance, this alphabet is alphabet's epitome, a star among alphabets, a national treasure for Koreans and "one of the great intellectual achievements of humankind", in the judgment of British linguist, Geoffrey Sampson.

— John Man, *Alpha Beta: How 26 Letters Shaped the Western World*[3]

The Korean alphabet Hangul, which today has become a visual ambassador for Korean culture, was created in 1443 by King Sejong. Three years later, it was set out in published form together with a manual explaining it in detail. Sejong named the alphabet and its accompanying volume Hunmin Chongum ("The proper Sounds for Instructing the People"). The Korean alphabet is nowadays commonly referred to as Hangul, which means the "Script of Han (Korea)" or the "Great Script."

Of the six thousand languages in existence today, only three hundred have their own alphabets. Of these three hundred languages, Hangul is the only

---

[3] John Man, *Alpha Beta: How 26 Letters Shaped the Western World* (New York: John Wiley & Songs, 2000), 108-109.

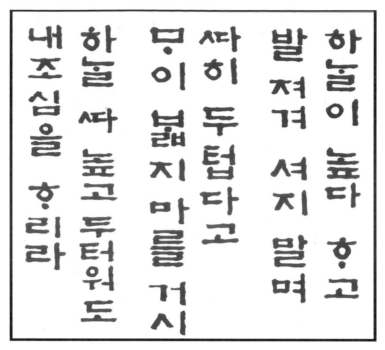

Hangul Calligraphy

alphabet whose inventor, theory, and motives behind its creation have been fully set out and explained. Roman characters have their origins in the hieroglyphics of Egypt and the syllabic Phoenician alphabets, and had to undergo a process of gradual evolution to become what they are today. Chinese characters, similarly, began as inscriptions on bones and tortoise shells, and took thousands of years to reach their current form.

However, Hangul is neither based on ancient written languages nor an imitation of another set of characters, but an alphabet unique to Korea. Moreover, as a highly scientific writing system, based on profound linguistic knowledge and philosophical principles, Hangul is practical and convenient as well as beautiful.

According to the Explanations and Examples of the Hunmin Chongum (1446), the basic consonant symbols were schematic drawings of the human speech organs in the process of articulating certain sounds, while the other consonants were formed by adding strokes to these five basic shapes.

The velar ㄱ (k) depicts the root of the tongue blocking the throat.

The alveolar ㄴ (n) depicts the outline of the tongue touching the upper palate.

The labial ㅁ (m) depicts the outline of the mouth.

The dental ㅅ (s) depicts the outline of the incisor.

The laryngeal ㅇ (zero initial) depicts the outline of the throat.

The pronunciation of the aspirated velar ㅋ (k') is more forceful than that of ㄱ (k), and therefore a stroke is added.

CONSONANTS OF THE KOREAN ALPHABET

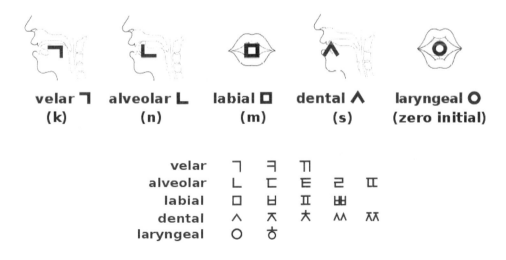

velar ㄱ	alveolar ㄴ	labial ㅁ	dental ㅅ	laryngeal ㅇ
(k)	(n)	(m)	(s)	(zero initial)

velar	ㄱ	ㅋ	ㄲ		
alveolar	ㄴ	ㄷ	ㅌ	ㄹ	ㄸ
labial	ㅁ	ㅂ	ㅍ	ㅃ	
dental	ㅅ	ㅈ	ㅊ	ㅆ	ㅉ
laryngeal	ㅇ	ㅎ			

43

The vowel symbols were formed according to the three fundamental symbols of Eastern philosophy.

The round · represents Heaven.

The flat ㅡ represents Earth.

The upright ㅣ represents Man.

These were the three basic vowels, and others were made by placing the round dot above or below the horizontal line, and to the left and right of the vertical line : ㅏ, ㅑ, ㅓ, ㅕ, ㅗ. ㅛ. ㅜ, ㅠ. The vowels therefore represent the harmony of heaven, earth and men.

The consonants and vowels each represent a phoneme, or unit of speech, and together the letters make a syllable. For example, "Moon" in Korean is "달" (dal), which consists of: ㄷ(consonant)+ㅏ(vowel)+ㄹ(consonant). In other words, Korean is both a phonemic and a syllabic language.

Hangul's qualities have fascinated modern-day scholars around the world. Robert Ramsey, a professor at Maryland University, described the originality of Hangul as follows:

The Korean alphabet is like no other writing system in the world. It is the only alphabet completely native to East Asia…The structure of the Korean alphabet shows a sophisticated understanding of phonological science that was not equaled in the West until modern times.[4]

---

[4] Robert Ramsey, "The Korean Alphabet," *King Sejong the Great,* ed. Young-Key Kim-Renaud (Seoul: Singu 1997), 198.

In his book Writing Systems: A Linguistic Introduction, British linguist Geoffrey Sampson devoted a special chapter to Hangul, and stated:

>...we may well marvel at the outstanding simplicity and convenience of Hangul. Whether or not it is ultimately the best of all conceivable scripts for Korean, Hangul must unquestionably rank as one of the great intellectual achievements of humankind.[5]

The praise of renowned scholars for this relatively young alphabet is seemingly without end. Professor Jared Diamond of UCLA, winner of the Pulitzer Prize in 1997 for his book Guns, Germs, and Steel, wrote an article entitled "Writing Right" for Discover magazine. In the article, he described Hangul as "an ultra-rational system" and "a precise reflection of a people's speech."[6] Some other scholars even attribute Korea's rapid economic development and growth in information technology during recent decades to Hangul, which has helped to keep illiteracy rates in Korea among the lowest in the world.

>The spoken language of our country is different from that of China and does not suit the Chinese characters. Therefore amongst uneducated people there have been many who, having something that they wish to put into words, have been unable to express their thoughts in writing. I am greatly distressed because of this, and so I have made twenty eight

[5] Geoffrey Sampson, *Writing Systems: A Linguistic Introduction* (Stanford: Stanford University Press, 1985), 144.
[6] Jared Diamond, "Writing Right," *Discover,* June 1994, 107, 109.

new letters. Let everyone practice them at their ease, and adapt them to their daily use.

– King Sejong's Preface to Hunmin Chongum (1446)

This passage, although short, clearly demonstrates the benevolent attitude of King Sejong the Great, who sincerely hoped that all people would learn how to read and write. Unfortunately, the circumstances of the day were not favorable for his new invention.

At the time, a call for universal literacy would have been highly out-of-the-ordinary. It would have been considered by many unnecessary and undesirable for the general population to be able to read. Some of those in power would even have thought it dangerous to put a tool as politically important as writing in the hands of the common people.

King Sejong's chief concern, however, was how best to educate his countrymen. Not only did he often write about the importance of literacy, but he also urged those who had been educated to do their best to teach others, and encouraged everyone – both women and men – to learn how to read. His passion was such that, while devoting himself to the creation of the Korean alphabet, Sejong almost lost his eyesight owing to the many late nights he spent at his desk.

Thanks to the new alphabet, the lives of ordinary people did, in time, dramatically change. People were able for the first time to write letters to their loved ones and gain knowledge by reading books. With an illiteracy rate of almost zero in Korea today, Koreans are still benefiting from the Sejong's determination and self-sacrifice.

In memory of King Sejong's noble spirit, Koreans commemorate Hangul Day as a national holiday every year on October 9th. UNESCO has also established the 'King Sejong Literacy Prize', annually awarded to individuals or groups that have made a significant contribution to the battle against global illiteracy.

Used now as an alternative alphabet for the world's minority peoples who have no written language, Sejong's invention continues to be a lamp for those without the gift of reading and writing. The Chepang Tribe from Nepal, who are without an alphabet of their own, have adopted the Korean letters Hangul in an effort to preserve their language and culture. Over in Indonesia, the Cia-Cia, a small ethnic group with a population of 60,000, has adopted Hangul as its alphabet for transcribing the aboriginal Austronesian language.

Linguists of the world acknowledge the originality and depth of Hangul, and its logical and pragmatic basis. More valuable than the alphabet itself, however, is the selfless love and devotion of Sejong that it embodies. His sincere wish that all people could learn to express their thoughts in writing is the true pride of Korea and a spiritual legacy to share with the whole world.

5. Scientific Progress in 15th Century Korea

During King Sejong's reign, a large number of noteworthy scientific achievements were made in Korea. The advances made in the disciplines of astronomy, meteorology, medicine, and printing are among the most ingenious and impressive in world history, and deserve recognition alongside other accomplishments in the Far East. As mentioned in the introduction, the Japanese Dictionary of Science and Technography, published in 1983, recorded that of the major scientific achievements of the period 1400-1450, 29 were made in Korea, 5 in China, and 28 in the rest of the world.[7]

Sejong's desire to increase agricultural output led to many inventions, such as the world's first rain gauge. Korea as a result possesses the longest systematic record of rainfall in the world, made possible by this device. Sejong also sought to raise the standard of farming methods in use at the time, publishing Nongsa Chiksol (A Plain Guide to Farming) in order to make the most efficient methods as widely known as possible. The spread of advanced farming techniques enabled continuous cultivation of the land for the first time in the history of the country.

Under Sejong, astronomical devices such as armillary spheres and sundials also improved, resulting in the publication of Chiljongsan (A Calculation of the Motions of the Seven Celestial Determinants; the Sun and Moon, Mercury, Mars, Jupiter, Venus and Saturn), a monumental work completed in 1442. In this book we find the length of a year calculated to be 365.2425 days, and one month as 29.530593 days – values correct to six significant figures according to today's estimates. With the help of the formulae contained in the book, astronomers were able to calculate the position of all the planets using the Korean capital as a reference point, as well as the exact time and occurrence of solar and lunar eclipses. The only other nations capable of making astronomical calculations to such a degree of accuracy were China and Arabia. Two hundred and forty years

---

[7] Sang-woon Jeon, "King Sejong the Great: The Leader of 15th Century Science Hist roy," *Twelve Historical Figures of Korean Science and Technology* (Seoul: Haenamu, 2005), 77.

later, the Chiljongsan was introduced to Japan by Royal ambassador Pak In-gi, enabling Japan to publish a native almanac compiled with respect to its own position.

King Sejong also reformed the medical system so that everyone would have equal access to medical care. He established public health clinics and medical schools, as well as national examinations to select the most talented and learned in the field. Before sitting the examination, prospective physicians were required to undergo a period of apprenticeship, in order to learn medical practice as well as theory.

Sejong made particular efforts to ensure that medical benefits were made available to everyone in his kingdom. He sent government doctors to remote areas such as Hamgyong Province in the far northeast and Cheju Island on the south-western coast. He also made medical textbooks available to scholars and students there, so that they would have an opportunity to study medical science formally. In Confucian society there was a strict distinction between male and female, and women were reluctant to be seen by a male doctor. Sejong recruited and educated female physicians so that female patients could receive better medical care before becoming seriously ill. He also extended his concern to those in prison, and arranged for the medical staff working in public clinics to rotate to prisons in order to provide them with a higher standard of care.

In 1445, a joint effort by the Chiphyonjon scholars and a committee of medical experts resulted in the publication of a medical encyclopaedia of 365 volumes, entitled Uibang Yuchwi (A Classified Collection of Medical Prescriptions). Due to the knowledge provided by such publications, there was a steep decline in infant mortality and an overall increase in population growth.

King Sejong promoted improvements in printing technology in order to provide vehicles of knowledge for the people. In Korea, the method of printing using wooden blocks (xylography) began in the 8th century, and movable metal type (typography) was used for the first time in 1234, some two hundred years before Gutenberg developed his famous printing press in Germany. In order to meet the demand for a great number and variety of printed texts, Sejong ordered his technicians to make typography more efficient. After much trial and error, they finally succeeded in developing a process that was faster and more economical, with a potential print run of 100 copies per day – a five-fold improvement on former models.

The King was also responsible for the invention of a variety of lead-based metal type. He and his technicians were aware that lead had a low melting point and cooled quickly, and was consequently well suited to be used for casting large-type publications for the elderly, whose failing eyesight made it difficult for them to read characters of a standard size.

Whenever a book was published, Sejong would hold a feast in great delight. Through his earnest desire to share the blessings of culture and literature with many, the art of printing in 15th century Korea took many great steps forward.

6. Sejong as a Reformer and Innovator

The society of 15th century Korea was strictly hierarchical, as was the case in the most of the world. Positions in government were open only to the nobility or yangban class. *Yang* means "two" or "both", and *ban* means seat, position, or status. The name was derived from the fact that in the royal court, officials were seated to the right and left of the king. Members of the yangban class married one another and lived apart from the other classes. In the capital of Hanyang – present day Seoul – their residences were in the northern and southern districts. Generally speaking, only members of this hereditary class were eligible to enter for the state examinations, the sole gateway to government office.

In Choson Korea, there were three types of state examination: literary, military and technical. Since proficiency in literary studies was more highly regarded than expertise in more practical areas such as law, medicine and foreign languages, the highest roles in government were awarded to those who had been successful in the literary examinations. However, entry for the literary state examinations was restricted to all but the offspring of a legal wife of a yangban.

The Class System of Choson Korea

Yangban ("The Right and Left") Scholars and Military Commanders
Chungin ("The Middle Men") Physicians, Inspectors, Auditors, Translators, Technicians and Others
Sangin ("The Commoners") The greater populace, consisting mainly of farmers
Chonin ("The Lesser Commoners") Private and public servants, professional entertainers, jesters, butchers, shamans and others

The children of a yangban's concubine could enter only for the technical examinations, and as a result such men generally went on to become professionals such as physicians, inspectors, auditors, translators, and technicians.

Those born to concubines in yangban households usually lived in the middle district of the capital, and were thus called chungin, or "middle men." While still considered in a broad sense to be part of the ruling class, the chungin were in fact treated very differently. In Choson society, those who worked in science and technology tended to be of chungin rank, and were invariably the victims of discrimination and repression when selections were being made for government posts. In the early 15th century, however, a large number of talented scientists were chosen for important government offices by King Sejong, who believed that ability and talent were more important than social status. The chungin promoted in this way received such favorable treatment that they found themselves drawing the envy of certain literary officials.

From time to time King Sejong would visit the Chomsong Observatory to hold discussions with the astronomers. When the talk was over, he would see that they were served fine wine. He promoted the scientists Yun Sa-ong, Yi Mu-rim, Choi Chon-gu, and Chong Yong-guk to the governorship of the districts surrounding Seoul, saying, "Having witnessed the hard work and effort of the officers of astronomy, I now bestow on them positions of responsibility in government, and I believe my intention is neither futile nor unwise." After this, the Royal Secretariat is said to have petitioned the king twice daily for several days: "Your Highness, there is no one who is not appalled by the prospect of several important provinces falling under the governance of a vulgar rabble, such as these men are. We beseech Your Highness to withdraw your decree with all haste." Sejong, however, refused to amend his order, and continued to praise the work and efforts of the astronomers.

The most notable example of Sejong's resolution to promote talent regardless of social rank is the case of Chang Yong-sil. His decision in this matter turned out to be very prudent. Chang, who later became famous for his invention of the sundial and automated water-clock, began his career as a servant in the government offices at Tongrae. According to the Sejong Sillok, his father was from Sohangju in China, and his mother was a kisaeng (professional entertainer) from Tongrae. Despite his lowly origin, he displayed an exceptional talent for engineering and mechanics. When he learned of Chang's gifts, Sejong sent him abroad so that he could familiarize himself with the most advanced scientific theories. After studying at various observatories, Chang was relieved of his servant status and appointed Royal Scientist in the seventh year of Sejong's reign (1425). When the decision for his appointment to office was first made known, opposition from several ministers temporarily halted proceedings altogether. When Taejong later added his support to Chang's case at the next discussion of his appointment, he was finally given the undisputed right to become an official of the Royal Household.

Having been raised from servant status to the rank of Royal Scientist within a single day, Chang continued to enjoy the favor of Sejong for the twenty years that followed. He went on to contribute to the design and construction of the celestial globe, the astrolabe, the sundial, the automatic water clock, and the rain gauge, many of which were the sole result of his own work. He also worked with Yi Chon to improve printing technology, and made a great many other contributions to the study of science before his death.

During Sejong's reign, many political reforms were undertaken. The changes made to the legal system are among the most noteworthy. Sejong was grieved that the majority of judicial officers gave judgment on a purely subjective basis rather than on grounds of evidence obtained through proper investigation. He was aware that many mistakes and failures were taking place within the justice system. Therefore, in the thirteenth year of his reign, he wrote and dispatched a letter of almost four thousand words, urging officers throughout the country to give fair and carefully measured verdicts.

Though he was eager that trials should be carried out fairly, Sejong's ultimate aspiration was a country that could exist without a penal system, and a harmonious society with empty prisons. Faced in reality with circumstances that required penal laws, Sejong often agonized greatly over verdicts when he was called to deliver them, and would lighten punishments as far as possible whenever he could. To reinforce the moral fabric of society, he improved the procedure for appeal and regulated the punishment system. The most important items of his reforms were as follows:

(1) In the case of offenses for which a specific legal provision is not available, the judge was instructed to apply analogous laws with caution. When passing the sentence, the death penalty was to be avoided wherever possible, and even lighter punishments applied with less severity.

(2) The rod used for official beatings was made according to standardised measurements, and the striking of certain parts of the body, such as the

backbone, was forbidden.

(3) In the case of crimes for which a fine could be paid in place of a punishment, the fines were reduced, and the lower classes were allowed to pay smaller fines in proportion to their income.

(4) The Law of Three Appeals: those accused of capital crimes were to be granted three opportunities to appeal to the king, so that no one would die with an unheard grievance.

(5) Pregnant women who were convicted would begin to serve their sentence only 100 days after giving birth.

(6) Except in cases of murder or robbery, those below the age of 15 or above the age of 70 were not to be imprisoned. Those below the age of 10 or above the age of 80 were not to be imprisoned under any circumstances.

(7) Those sentenced to penal servitude whose parents were above the age of 70 served their sentence in the region where their parents were living.

(8) Officials guilty of accepting bribes of any kind were no longer to be pardoned.

(9) When a slave-owner beat or killed his slave in private, he was to be punished according to the law.

(10) Constant efforts were made to ensure that no one was placed in custody for an unduly long period of time because of delays in the legal process.

(11) Architectural designs for new prisons were drawn up under the King's supervision, and construction began across the country. Separate prisons were built for women and men, cooler prisons for spring and summer, and warmer prisons for the fall and winter period. Prisoners were also allowed to bathe once a week.

7. Altruism in Governance

Sejong firmly believed that it was the duty and mission of a king to serve his country as well as he possibly could, and to sacrifice himself for the sake of its people. The people's happiness was the sole standard against which he measured his success as ruler. Furthermore, Sejong's love for his people was not confined to a particular class. When we consider his warm compassion for the young and old, his concern for the rights of slaves and prisoners, his welfare policies, and his openness to the peoples of other nations, it seems incredible that his was an era in which kings were more commonly cruel and brutal oppressors of their countrymen.

This chapter contains extracts from the Sillok, or Annals of the Choson Dynasty. They give examples of Sejong's words and actions, and an insight into the character and spirit of a true altruistic leader.

5 February, 3rd year of Sejong's Reign

By Royal Order,

"The continuous flooding and drought of recent times has led to successive years of bad harvests. This last year has been particularly severe, and the lives of the people have become wretched. The Governor and the Chief Administrator of each province must provide relief for all, giving priority to the sick and handicapped. In due course, an official from the central government will tour and inspect the various districts. If it is discovered that there is one person who has died from starvation in the residential district of any province, the official responsible for that province will be convicted of felony."

3 July, 5th year

The King said,

"The common people are the foundation of any country. It is only when this foundation is strong that a country will be stable and prosperous."

20 June, 7th year

The King said,

"The courtiers and officials will keep in mind the hardships of the people, and endeavor to point out every one of my faults, as well as errors and oversights in my ordinances and commands, so that I may fear the Heavens and have the utmost regard for the wellbeing of the people."

28 July, 7th year

For the past ten days, since the 18th of the month, the King has stayed awake until dawn out of concern because of the drought. He has become ill as a result, but has forbidden that his illness be announced to the public.

23 February, 10th year

To the inspectors who were leaving to investigate reports of starvation in their provinces, the King said,

"Go in person to the hamlets hidden in the hills and the mountains, and if you come across a person in hunger, give him rice, beans, salt and soy sauce, and save his life. If a local governor has hidden anyone who has died or suffered from malnutrition, you must punish him according to the disciplinary laws. If his position is equal to or higher than 3 pum[8], you must first inform the Central Government. If his position is equal to or less than 4 pum, you may judge his offence there and then. If the need for relief is urgent, open the storehouses yourselves and give the people relief. "

5 November, 1st year

When the mother of the exile Kim Han-ro passed away, the King said,

"Returning home to attend the funeral of one's parent is an obligation in keeping with natural law and with human nature. Moreover, since the former king has already given the order, I must abide by it. It would be no great offense for Kim Han-ro to take care of the funeral, provided that he returns to his place of exile after doing so."

The courtiers petitioned the King two or three times, alleging that it would

---

[8] All government officials, both civil and military, were given ranks from 1 *pum* to 9 *pum*, with 1 *pum* being the highest level. Each *pum* was divided into two ranks: t here were thus 18 ranks all together.

not be right to allow a criminal to return from exile. The King did not listen to their recommendations and summoned Kim Han-ro home together with his son Kim Kyung-jae to oversee his mother's funeral.

7 April, 5th Year

The King ordered the royal family to pour wine for one another. When the turn came for Prince Hyoryong [King Sejong's elder brother] to pour wine for the King, the King stood up to receive it.

Two envoys from China later asked Hwang Hee, "At today's banquet, why did the King stand to receive wine from Prince Hyoryong?"

Hwang Hee replied, "If you think of His Majesty and Prince Hyoryong as a king and his subject, he was under no obligation to stand. The reason that the King stood up was because he regards it as his duty to respect his elder brother."

The envoys were moved by the King's actions and praised his virtue highly.

11 May, 4th year

Yon Sa-chong and Pyon Kye-ryang said to the King, "Ever since Your Majesty began to tend the former king at his sickbed, no food has passed your lips. We are concerned that you may damage your health."

The King said, "The Six Ministries delivered a similar message yesterday, and now that you have added your concerns, I will dine this evening."

After an evening ceremony, the officials of the central government and Six Ministries came before the king in tears, "Your Majesty has not eaten anything since the former king's illness worsened. An ancient sage taught, 'The living should not harm their health for the sake of the dead.' Your Majesty, please restrain your grief and eat so that you may truly fulfill your duty of love towards the former king."

The King then began to eat thin gruel once a day.

11 February, 5th year

A Royal Ordinance was issued as follows:

"From now on, any soldier who wishes to visit his sick parents should be granted leave immediately, and should not be required to submit an official report until later. Let this practice be followed from now on."

29 September, 14th year

When his horse ate a handful of rice from a farmer's storehouse, the King said, "The farmer has taken great troubles to farm this rice, and since my horse has eaten it, he should receive what would have been due to him." He then ordered that the farmer be given a sack of rice in recompense.

15 November, 31st year

The King said to Yi Kye-jon,

"In the Year of the Serpent [the 7th Year of the King's reign, a year of severe drought], my illness became so grave and my chances of survival so slight that a coffin was prepared for me."

7 May, 3rd year

The King had ordered two rooms to be built using discarded timber from the eastern part of the Kyonghoe Hall. The stairways were not to be made of stone, the roof was to be covered with straw, and only simple decorations were used, according to the King's request. When the new chambers were built, he no longer used his old offices, but stayed in these new rooms instead.

19 April, 7th year

The King said,

"Appreciation of the good must be long-lasting; hatred for the bad must not."

26 March, 11th year

The officer Chong Yon said,

"Yesterday, a man leapt in front of Your Majesty's carriage. According to the laws, he should be executed."

The King replied,

"This is most unjust. If he jumped in full awareness of the law, the rule should be applied as you have said. But to punish an ignorant person who acted out of bewilderment, not knowing his way, is not right."

25 February, 14th year

While the King's ostler was on guard in the mountains, a large wild boar, struck with many arrows, managed to break through the fence and charged into the King's horse, killing it. The officers Choi Yun-dok and Chong Yon declared,

"In their neglect, the palace staff have allowed the Royal horse to be killed. We request that Your Majesty permit their offence to be judged."

The King replied,

"It happened quite unexpectedly. How could they have known that a large boar would run into this particular horse? Do not speak of this again."

19 October, 12th year

The King said to his Secretaries,

"In the past, when a government servant gave birth, she was expected to return to service after seven days. This provision was made out of concern for the fact that harm might come to the baby if she returned to her work leaving the child behind, and so this period of leave was later increased to a hundred days. However, there have been instances of women whose time was near, and who gave birth before reaching home. I therefore suggest that one month of full leave be granted prior to giving birth. Please amend the relevant laws."

26 April, 16th year

Dispatched to the Ministry of Justice:

"It has been enacted that a female servant, who is due to give birth in a month's time or who has given birth within the past hundred days, shall not be required for government service. Since no leave has been granted to the husbands of such women, however, they have not been able to provide assistance to their wives in childbirth. Because of this some women have lost their lives, and this is most pitiful. From this day forward, a husband is not required to return to service for thirty days after his wife has given birth."

1 May, 7th year

The King ordered the Ministry of Justice:

"The purpose of a prison is to punish those who have committed crimes, not to be a place in which they are left to die.   However, the officials in charge of prisons, instead of sincerely caring for those in their charge, sometimes incarcerate men in extremely cold or hot weather, causing them to become ill or to freeze and die. This is most unfortunate and deserving of our pity. In deference to this most sincere wish of mine, let the officials of both central and provincial governments make a habit of inspecting the prisons personally, and seeing that they are kept in good repair and in an ordered state. They should also provide the sick prisoners with medicine. For the prisoners who do not have families to bring them supplies, the government must give them food and clothes. Officials who do not faithfully carry out these directives will be strictly supervised and punished by the Office of the Inspector General in Seoul and by the Governors in Provinces."

27 November, 12th year

A Royal Ordinance to the Ministry of Justice:

"To be imprisoned and tortured is an ordeal for any man. In the case of children and the elderly, it is pitiful indeed. From this day forward, the detention of those aged below 15 or above 70 is forbidden, unless the charge is one of murder or robbery. Persons below the age of 10 or above the age of 80 shall under no circumstances be detained or beaten, and any verdict passed in their case must be given on the basis of many testimonies. Let this Ordinance be known throughout the country, and anyone in breach of it be punished."

24 March, 12th year

A man named Choi Yu-won beat one of his slaves to death. The King ordered the Ministry of Justice to bring him to trial, declaring,

"Even though a man is a slave, he is no less a man, and even if he has sinned, to punish him with death in private and without the sanction of the law is to disregard a master's duty to love and care for his servant. This man should therefore be brought to trial for his offense."

28 July, 13th year

A Royal Ordinance to the Ministry of Justice:

"When a person who is unmarried commits a crime and is imprisoned, his or her young children may die from cold and starvation if no one cares for them. From now on, let such children be taken to their relatives. Babies that still require breastfeeding shall be given to those who can accommodate them.

If the children do not have relatives, the local government office should take custody of the children and raise them. The officials of the local governments should bring them up with the utmost care. If they fail to do so and the children suffer from cold weather and starvation, the Office of the General Inspector and Governors of the Provinces will investigate and discipline those responsible."

2 July, 30th year

The King said,

"In the past, I have not been troubled by the heat. As the climate has grown more extreme in recent years, I have begun to soak my hands in water during hot weather. When I do so, the feeling of heat immediately disappears. This has led me to reflect how easy it must be for a man in a prison to be affected by the heat. Some, I believe, even lose their lives because of it, and this is greatly distressing.

When there is very hot weather, let us place small jars of water in the cells of the prisons, and replace the water frequently, directing the prisoners to wash their hands so that they are not affected by the heat."

28 January, 16th year

Sin Sang, an official from the Ministry of Rites, reported,

"The Alta tribe of the Jurchens have submitted this message to the Royal Court, 'We understand that you have established a military base in the region of Hwaeryong, and wish to know whether you will allow us to live in peace with you as before, or intend to drive us away.' I believe, Your Highness, that it is their genuine wish to settle with us in peace."

And the king responded,

"If they wish to become part of our nation, we cannot drive them away, and if they wish to leave, there is no need for us to prevent it. Our establishment of a military base will not please them, but it cannot be denied that the rural district of Hwaeryong is our rightful possession.

Tongmaeng Kachop Moga [the chief of the Jurchens] once leased the land from us, but after his tribe was defeated by the rival Oljokhap, the region became desolate and empty, and so now we have been compelled to establish a military camp there to keep the peace. Other Jurchens have settled in Hamgil Province, and if the Alta tribe wishes to come and live in our country, it would be unjust to discriminate against them."

16 June, 24th year

The King said to several of his Secretaries,

"Ever since I came to the throne, I have thought nothing more worthy of diligent effort than consideration of the affairs of state. Therefore, I have held councils every day to debate and discuss issues of national importance. Through these, I have met with many officials each day, and have given my personal attention to state affairs, dealing with them individually. For this reason, the delivery of sentences has never been delayed, and no important matter has been left unheard."

22 February, 32nd year

The King would rise at dawn every day, and hear debriefings from his Ministers at daybreak. He would then consider general matters, and hold a council to determine the principles of governance. He would personally interview the governors as they left for their provinces. He participated in the Kyong-yon in order to reflect upon the Literature of the Sages and hold discussions about past and present events. Later, he would go to read in the Royal Chamber, and would not set down his book before retiring late at night.

8.   The Everlasting Light of Korea

Unlike many other kings given the title "Great" by posterity, Sejong's greatness did not stem from brute force or in the conquering and subduing of other peoples, but in a series of intellectual and cultural achievements that have continued to benefit his nation throughout many generations, and enrich the lives of people today.

Royal Tomb of King Sejong

Through his intelligence, creative energy, compassion, and good judgment, the King worked with untiring dedication to free his countrymen from poverty, injustice, and ignorance. He surrounded himself with capable scholars and scientists, whose ingenuity found an ordered and splendid means of expression under his leadership.

It is for this reason that the name of Sejong is given to many streets, schools, research institutes, cultural centers, and even businesses in modern Korea. Over time, he has come to win the respect and admiration of those outside Korea as well. The American linguist Dr. Macaulay has been celebrating Hangul Day for the past 30 years. On October 9 of every year, he prepares Korean food and invites his colleagues, students, and close friends to celebrate the creation of the Korean alphabet. Japanese scientist Watanabe Gatso of the International Astronomical Union chose to name a minor planet that he had discovered "7365 Sejong 1996 QV." And in Warsaw, Poland, one of the leading high schools has recently changed its name to Sejong High School and added the Korean language to its curriculum.

Sejong was a king who served the people with reverence and humility, who promoted the power and beauty of culture out of love and benevolence, and instilled in his country a new sense of independence and cultural identity. He possessed a deep respect for history and tradition, valued learning and scholarship, and led his country forward with bold and innovative reforms. Dressed in patched clothing and living beneath a humble roof, he never faltered in his sense of duty and responsibility even in the days when his work on the alphabet caused him to become almost blind. He was a father to the poor, the weak, the ignorant, and even wrongdoers and criminals.

Sejong, the fourth and greatest monarch of Choson Korea, continued after his death to be a deep root and inexhaustible spring for the Korean people. Despite the many words that have been written about this man, and may in future be written, his virtues can never be described in full.

References

Historical sources

Royal Annals of Choson Dynastty: Sejong Sillok

Other sources

Bae, Kichan. *Korea at the Crossroads: The History and Future of East Asia.* Seoul: Wisdom House, 2005.

Diamond, Jared. "Writing Right." *Discovery.* June, 1994.

Jeon, Sang-woon. *Science under King Sejong.* Seoul: King Sejong Memorial Society, 1986.

———. *A History of Science in Korea.* Seoul: Science Books, 2000.

———. "King Sejong the Great: The Leader of 15th Century Science History," *Twelve Historical Figures of Korean Science and Technology.* Seoul: Haenamu, 2005.

Kim, Ho. *Scientist of Choson Korea.* Seoul: Humanist, 2003.

Kim, Jung-soo. *The History and Future of Hangul.* Seoul: Youl Hwa Dang, 1990.

Kim-Renaud,Young-key. *King Sejong the Great: The Light of 15th Century Korea.* Seoul: Singu Munhwa Publications, 1998.

Kown, Yon-woong. "Kyong-yon and Confucianism in the Reign of King Sejong," *A Study of Culture in the Reign of King Sejong.* Seongnam: The Academy of Korean Studies, 1982.

Ledyard, Gari. "The Korean Language Reform of 1446: The Origin, Background, and Early History of the Korean Alphabet." Ph. D. Dissertation. University of California, Berkeley, 1966.

Man, John. *Alpha Beta: How 26 Letters Shaped the Western World*, New York: John Wiley & Songs, 2000.

Pak, Pyong-ho. *Legal Systems under King Sejong*, King Sejong Memorial Society, 1986.

Pak, Song-rae. "How the Chugugi became the Chinese Invention," *History for Tomorrow*, Vol. 18, 2004.

Sampson, Geoffrey. *Writing Systems: A Linguistic Introduction*. Stanford: Stanford University Press, 1985.

Sohn, Pokee. *Metal Type Printing*. Seoul: King Sejong the Great Memorial Society, 2000.

The Academy of Korean Studies, *Culture under King Sejong*, Taehak Publications, 2002.

Yi, Hwa-hyong. *Humanism: The Power of Korean Culture*, Kookhak, 2004.

Shin Saimdang: A Lady of Virtue and the Arts

There have been numerous painters since ancient times, yet the paintings of those whose virtue can be passed down to later generations are precious indeed. Often, paintings are separate from the morality of the painter. With her exemplary conduct, the Lady [Shin Saimdang] is outstanding even among the most distinguished women of this country.

> – From a foreword to Shin Saimdang's painting book
> by the scholar Song Sang-gi (1713)

1. Life and Education of Shin Saimdang

Shin Saimdang (1504~1551) was not only a scholar well versed in the Confucian classics and other great works of the literary tradition, but also an artist of fine distinction deeply admired by later generations as well as her contemporaries. Her case is indeed exceptional, as educational opportunities for women were very limited during the Choson Dynasty (1392~1910).

Portrait of Shin Saimdang

Shin Saimdang was born on October 29th in 1504 at Ojukheon ("house of black bamboo trees") in Gangneung, which was then her maternal grandparents' house. Saimdang's mother was an only child and continued to live with her parents after marriage, and Saimdang therefore grew up in the house of her maternal grandparents. Saimdang's parents had no sons, and she was the second eldest of five daughters. Her father, Shin Myungwha, lived mainly at his residence in Seoul, making frequent visits to his wife and children in Gangneung. For this reason, Saimdang and her sisters were influenced greatly by their maternal grandparents as well as their parents.

Until the mid-Choson Dynasty, the matrilocal custom was still prevalent – after marriage, a couple would reside with the parents of the wife for a certain period of time. If a daughter was an only child, she would continue the family line, and her descendants would hold memorial services for their maternal ancestors.[9] Saimdang grew up in her maternal grandparents' house, relatively free from the patriarchal order of the larger society. It was significant that Saimdang did not have any male siblings, as it meant that she was in a position to fully assume the intellectual inheritance of her father and maternal grandfather.

While growing up, Saimdang received an excellent education in literature, philosophy and art, studying at home rather than in school. She began learning to read and write at the age of four, and soon after that began calligraphy and painting, as well as embroidery. Her father Shin Myungwha would borrow famous paintings so that Saimdang could practice by copying them. At six, Saimdang surprised her family and relatives by making a near perfect replica of a landscape painting by An Kyon, who was a renowned painter of the early Choson period. In this nurturing environment, Saimdang could develop her intellect and artistic talents far beyond what was expected of women in the day.

---

[9] In the late Choson Dynasty (17th century onwards), the custom of matrilocality became less common and matrilineal ancestry was virtually abandoned in geneal ogy and memorial ceremonies.

From her mother, Saimdang learned how to practice virtuous conduct in her daily life, and how to teach her own children. Saimdang's father once became ill on his way from Seoul to his family in Gangneung. No medicine was effective, and he was between life and death. Saimdang's mother offered prayers for seven days and nights, but to no avail. She performed her ablutions and went up to grave of one of her ancestors. Here she made an altar, and cut off the half of her left middle finger as a sacrifice. She then prayed her utmost sincerity for her husband's recovery. Meanwhile, Saimdang, then aged 18, was nursing her father. As she drowsed for a moment, she had a dream in which a divine person gave heavenly medicine to her father. After this, her father miraculously recovered. All the people in the village believed that the Heavens had been moved by the prayer of Saimdang's mother and honored her wish. This became known outside the village, and seven years later, Saimdang's mother was awarded a monument of virtue[10] by the royal court. Saimdang took her mother as a role model to emulate, in particular for her love and perseverance.

Saimdang's father, Shin Myungwha, was also known for integrity and moral courage. When he passed the state examination for government service at the age of 41, his colleagues in the court tried to have him recommended for an official post, but he declined. During the era of King Yonsan and King Chungjong, there were two historical crises involving the scholars, as a result of which many were put to death for their philosophical and ideological

---

[10] During the Choson Dynasty, a monument of virtue was awarded to women who showed exemplary moral conduct as wife and mother, with the aim of instilling the Confucian values in ordinary people.

views. Shin Myungwha was deeply disillusioned with the times, and hence devoted himself to the pursuit of learning rather than the path of government.

When Saimdang reached the age of 19, she was married to Yi Wonsu. Yi grew up in Seoul, raised alone by his mother, and was her senior by three years. Directly after the wedding, Saimdang's father said to his son-in-law, "When all my many daughters are married, your wife is the only one that I will miss. It is hard indeed for me to part with her." This demonstrated the deep affection Saimdang's parents had for her. However, just several months after the wedding, her father passed away, while Saimdang was still living at her parents' house. With her mother alone, Saimdang could not leave for the in-law's residence in Seoul. She thus lived at Ojukheon for three more years to complete the mourning rites[11] for her father. Over the next ten years, she lived in both places by turns. At the age of 38, she succeeded her mother-in-law to take on the whole responsibility of the Seoul residence.

Unfortunately Saimdang did not live a long life. She passed away on May 17th in 1551, when she was only 46 years old. And yet, she had already achieved great renown, both in her deeds and in her art. Her achievements took on a tangible form in her art works, and could be seen also in the character of her children. She brought up four sons and three daughters. Among them, the eldest daughter, Maechang, and fourth son, Wu (courtesy name, Oksan), took after her artistically. The third son, Yi (courtesy name,

---

[11] In the Confucian tradition of the Choson Dynasty, when a parent passed away, the mourning period for the children of the deceased was three years. Strictly s peaking, the mourner was supposed to live in a hut near the burial site, observin g many restrictions on behavior and appearance.

Yulgok), became one of the most significant figures in Korean history, as a scholar, philosopher, and public servant.

2. The Meaning of the Courtesy Name, Saimdang

Saimdang's given name was Inseon, which means "generosity" ("in") and "goodness" ("seon"). However, she is better known by her courtesy name "Saimdang." A courtesy name is a name that one chooses oneself as a mark of one's individual and social identity. In the patriarchal hierarchy of the Choson society, having a courtesy name was a privilege granted to male aristocrats only. In case of women, whether common or noble, even given names were seldom used, and still fewer women had a courtesy name. We can therefore see that Saimdang had both the aptitude and determination to shape her identity beyond the customary boundaries of her society. She made an effort to overcome the limitations that society imposed on women, in order to realize her intellectual and artistic potential.

At the same time, however, her courtesy name tells that she aspired to live up to the ideals of womanhood in the Confucian tradition. The name "Saimdang" means "respecting Im as teacher" or "emulating Im." "Im" refers to Tae-Im, who was the mother of the King Mun in Chu, the ancient kingdom of China. Tae-Im was firm yet gentle, loving yet just, and considered to be an ideal woman in Confucian thought. The Book of Odes[12] contains a poem that

---

[12] One of the Three Classics of Ancient China, which consist of the Book of Od

describes her:

> Tae-Im is indeed worth of praise,
>
> The mother of King Mun …
>
> One who obeys her ancestors,
>
> Satisfies the gods,
>
> Pleases the spirits,
>
> Shows decency to queens,
>
> Offers grace to siblings.
>
> Thus she guided this country,
>
> Thoughtful in the court,
>
> Dignified in the temple,
>
> Prudent even when alone,
>
> Ever following the way
>
> That Heaven shows to mankind.

By her courtesy name, Saimdang indicated what she felt she should strive towards and put into practice. When later ages appraised her art and found her character reflected in it, it was clear that the courtesy name was indeed a guiding force in Saimdang's life and art.

---

es, the Canon of History, and the Book of Changes.

3. A Wise and Resolute Wife

Saimdang's husband, Yi Wonsu, was raised as an only son by his mother, his father having passed away early in his life. He had not the educational opportunities that Saimdang enjoyed, and in character he was somewhat indecisive. Naturally Saimdang was an example to him of scholarship, artistic excellence, and moral character. Yulgok, the third son, wrote as follows[13]:

> Father, a man of no mean caliber, did not apply himself to the minute details of running the household. We were not affluent, and Mother saved in every way she could, to provide for all the members of the house. She consulted with her mother-in-law, Lady Hong, about each and every matter. Even when speaking to servants, her voice was gentle and her demeanor was kind. When Father made a mistake, she would raise the issue with him personally. She disciplined her children and advised her juniors with consideration and consistency. For this reason, every person respected her.

Two episodes speak of the wise and resolute way in which Saimdang managed her household. The first is from the time when Saimdang was living in Gangneung after her wedding. Although she had attained a high level of scholarship in literature and art thanks to the attention of her father and

---

[13] Yulgok wrote "A Record of Late Mother's Life," directly following the death of his mother.

78

maternal grandfather, her husband had not, and she could not help being somewhat frustrated with his lack of education. One day, Saimdang suggested to him that he live apart from her for ten years, during which time he should devote himself to learning. This suggestion stemmed from her wish to help her husband make a meaningful contribution to society. Yi Wonsu reluctantly agreed.

He left for Seoul, leaving his wife behind at Gangneung. She said to him as he departed, "Please go, and devote yourself to study. Then, in ten years time, take your place in the world." Despite her firm directions, Yi travelled only five miles from Ojukheon before losing heart and returning. On the second day, he went seven and a half miles, and on the third day, ten miles.

In deep sorrow and disappointment, Saimdang said, "You, a man, have expressed an aim in life, and a determination to leave your home to achieve it. But each day you return to me. How could such a person ever make his way?" "Learning is important," her husband replied, "But I cannot live for ten years apart from you. A single moment without you is more than I can bear."

To coax him out of this sluggish and weak-minded mood, Saimdang resorted to drastic measures. She took a pair of scissors from her needle work basket and said, "If you are feeble and inconstant, I have no hope in life nor any reason to live. I will cut off my hair and flee to the mountains to become a nun. Or else – Heaven forgive me for my impiety – I will kill myself and end my wretched life here and now." Yi Wonsu was deeply moved by his wife's resolution, and finally made up his mind to go.

On the next day, he went to Seoul to focus on his studies. His resolution lasted for three years, after which he returned frequently to Gangneung to be with his wife. In the end, he did not achieve much in his studies. Before Saimdang died, he did advance to an official post, although a fairly modest one.

The second episode is from the time when Yi Wonsu's uncle, Yi Ki, held one of the highest positions in the royal court. Yi Ki was responsible for the great purge of scholars in 1545, during which many innocent men were killed. Following this, he ascended to a supreme position, and enjoyed great political support. Yi Wonsu was among his followers and made frequent calls on his uncle. Upon learning this, Saimdang strongly warned her husband against it, telling him, "You should not chase power, however splendid it may seem. The power of Yi Ki will be short-lived."

"He and I are of the same lineage," her husband replied, "And he is my great-uncle's son, therefore my uncle."

"Even if he belongs to the same family line, we should not set foot in his house knowing that he is not a man of upright deeds." Saimdang said firmly. "He led a plot to kill innocent scholars, and is now greedily pursuing power and acclaim. It will not be long before his time is over." Yi Wonsu had no choice but to agree with her, and so stopped his visits to Yi Ki. Thanks to Saimdang's insight and her sense of right, Yi Wonsu evaded the political turmoil that engulfed Yi Ki's followers when he later fell disgraced.

4. Educating Her Children

So as not to neglect her role as teacher to her children, Saimdang never travelled anywhere far from home. Yulgok and his siblings learned from their mother the philosophical principles of great scholars as well as the social customs and moral precepts of Confucianism. They also learned to compose both poetry and prose from a young age.

While Saimdang took the cultivation of the moral mind as the ultimate purpose of her children's education, she also prepared them to be able to serve the country. According to her teaching, "When one reads, one should always regard the great thinkers and wise men. When one is in an official post, one should always regard the king and the nation." Saimdang emphasized the importance of integrity and justice, and so it is no coincidence that Yulgok later had the courage to offer critical advice to the king, and to attempt many reforms to improve the living conditions of the public. The character and accomplishments of Saimdang's children bear witness to her earnest care for their education. Among four sons and three daughters, the accomplishments of the eldest daughter Maechang, third son Yi, and fourth son Wu have been recorded in most detail.

Yi Yi (courtesy name Yulgok) proved his genius early on in life by winning first place nine times in the state examination for government service. He later developed profound, distinctive and compelling philosophical views and political ideas. Together with Yi Hwang, he was one of the two most influential Confucian thinkers in the Choson Dynasty. His writings contributed significantly to the development of Confucian philosophy and thought in the mid-Dynasty period. He entered government service at the age of 29 and worked in various positions until his death at twenty years later. While in the public service, he initiated many reform proposals. For instance, he proposed that government posts be opened up to everyone regardless of class and social status. He also proposed that the obligations of tax and army service be applied equally and fairly to everybody, without the privilege of exemption for certain groups or classes. When he was the Minister of Defense, he saw that the international politics around the Korean peninsula would escalate into a full-scale war. He paid particular attention to the military aspirations of Hideyoshi's regime in Japan, and strongly recommended that Choson train 100,000 soldiers in preparation for an enemy invasion. Following the teachings of his mother, Yulgok worked with his earnest sincerity to realize the principles of Confucianism, and put into practice the idea of the "king-as-philosopher," in order to solve the social and political dilemmas of his day. It was indeed a great loss to Korea that Yulgok's proposal for national defense was not accepted. Eight years after he passed away, Hideyoshi invaded Korea and the country was overcome and devastated.

Saimdang's eldest daughter, Maechang, took after Saimdang in many respects. She was not only knowledgeable in history and the classics, but also talented in poetry, calligraphy, and painting, as her mother had been. Her compassion and intelligence led others to refer to her as a second Saimdang. Speaking of her work, a critic remarked, "The mood of her poetry is fresh and pure, and the paintings are skillful and intricate."[14]

Yulgok would often consult with his eldest sister on political or government matters. A story goes that when Yulgok was the Minister of Defense, there was a disturbance at the Northern Border. Yulgok was concerned that the Choson Border Guard were short of provisions, and Maechang said to her brother, "The most urgent task is to act as the public would wish. Currently, the son of a concubine cannot enter government service, regardless of his ability, and so naturally such men are greatly resentful. If they are allowed to take the government service exam in exchange for a payment of rice, they will be content with the opportunity, and the payment can be used to feed the army." Yulgok was impressed with her suggestion, and appealed to the King to adopt the new idea.

The fourth son, Yi Wu (courtesy name, Oksan), was decorated by the court for his outstanding service during Hideyoshi's invasion. During the war, he was responsible for the County if Koesan, and organized a volunteer army to resist the Japanese. At the same time, he collected and made shrewd use of intelligence about enemy movements, so that he was able to direct the farmers in the various provinces to time their crop-growing accordingly, and the entire county thus avoided famine. At another time, he served as the head of Village Bian. After finishing his official term there, he worked in the village for another seven years at the request of the officials and residents of the village. Moreover, Oksan was highly gifted in Komungo (a six-string

---

[14] From "Foreword to the Family Painting Book", by Yi Suh, a descendant of Yi Wu.

Korean harp), calligraphy, poetry, and painting. Together with his sister Maechang, Oksan carried on the family's artistic tradition. Hwang Kiro, Oksan's father-in-law and a leading figure in cursive style calligraphy, once declared, "Compared with my own calligraphy, his work may not be as elegant, but shows greater spirit."[15] Yulgok was very close to Oksan, and once said, "If my brother Wu had devoted himself to learning, my achievements would be second to his." As with Maechang, we are fortunate that some of Oksan's poetry, calligraphy, and paintings have been preserved and can be appreciated today.

The lives of Saimdang's children are a vivid testament to the fact that their education by Saimdang was not one merely of ideas, but of practical application. The children held foremost the Confucian maxim "The first task is to discipline oneself. The second is to serve others."

5. Saimdang, the Artist

Before all else, Saimdang was an artist. She was a person of great sensitivity. One day, she was listening to a performance by a maid from the household of one of her relatives, who was playing the Komungo. Upon hearing the tune, Saimdang was deeply affected and shed tears, leading the other guests to contemplate their own sorrows.

Of her artistic output, two poems, seven calligraphic works, and forty

---

[15] Taken from the "Foreword to the Family Painting Book."

paintings remain. Both of the poems are addressed to her mother. One of them was written in the Great Pass of Daegwanryong, while on her way to Seoul to take up her housekeeping duties at the residence of her in-laws, at the age of 38. This was an important point in her life, as it signified that she was leaving her birthplace and mother completely.

At the Great Daegwanryong Pass

> My aged mother is left behind in my former home,
> While I am on a lonely road to Seoul.
> The northern village is far away,
> Only clouds are flowing over in the sunset.

Another poem was written in Seoul, expressing her affection for her mother and feelings of homesickness. Saimdang would often stay up all night in tears, missing her mother who was living alone. Yulgok wrote,[16] "The home in Gangneung was constantly in Mother's thoughts. Often she would carry her sorrows deep into the night, with silent tears, in the quiet of the darkness. Sometimes her vigils would last all night." Her sensitivity and filial devotion alone are insufficient explanation for this behavior. It is highly likely that she had inner sorrows that she endured privately, not confiding in others. Her poems reveal the depth of her emotions and yearning.

---

[16] "A Record of Late Mother's Life."

Thinking of Mother

Although thousands of miles away,

Far over hills and mountains,

Day and night I spend in longing.

The lonesome moon by the Pine Tree Pavilion,

A gentle breeze at the Gyungpo Shore.

On the sands, sea gulls scatter and gather,

On the sea, the fishing boats come and go.

Will I ever come home to Gangneung again,

And sit by my mother, enjoying needlework?

Saimdang achieved a high level of proficiency in calligraphy as well as in poetry. A critic[17] of a later age remarked, "Her brushstrokes are made with sincerity. They are calm and profound, elegant and chaste. One can see clearly that the Lady Shin took after King Mun's mother, Tae-Im." Another critic[18] wrote, "If one carefully appraises the Lady Shin's writing, one comes to acquire a deep admiration for the mother who raised her son [Yulgok]." These commentaries observe that Saimdang's calligraphic writing is itself an eloquent expression of her cultivated mind.

Saimdang's artistic gifts are exhibited most strikingly in her paintings, which express her delicate feeling, warmth and candor. Part of Saimdang's

---

[17] Yoon Jongeui, the head of Gangneung District, made this remark in 1869, after engraving an example of Saimdang's calligraphy on a wooden plaque, kept in Ojuheon.
[18] Yi Hyunggyu, then head of Gangneung District, wrote a foreword to Saimdang's calligraphy screen work, in 1774.

method was to use color from the beginning, without first drawing visible outlines. For the subjects of her paintings, she chose everyday things such as flowers, small plants, insects, and birds. By means of her affectionate and exquisite brushstrokes, these modest and humble subjects took on a new life once painted. With the utmost skill, she captured even minute details such as the veins of a leaf, the stamen of a flower, and the wings and legs of insects. Her powers of observation were thorough and exact. It is related that when she placed a painting of grass insects to dry under the sun, a hen attempted to eat them, piercing the paper several times with its beak.

A wide variety of objects appear in Saimdang's paintings. Among insects, we find depictions of crickets, bees, dragonflies, and cicadas. Among other small creatures, we find worms, ants, mice, lizards, and toads. Among plants, bellflowers, pinks, cockscombs, poppies, cucumbers, water melons, ground cherries, and eggplants. Mice are seen nibbling at the fruits, while a beetle is seen rolling a ball of cow dung, and a praying mantis stands in mid-motion. These well-observed and entertaining scenes could not have been made without a sense of humor and warmth towards nature.

Saimdang was particularly famous for her grape paintings. One day when she was staying in Gangneung, she was invited to a party with some other ladies. A younger member of the group happened to spill some tea on her skirt. The lady was distraught, as she had borrowed the skirt from someone else. Saimdang had asked her to spread the skirt on the floor, and painted a large grape leaf over the stain. She then drew other leaves and bunches of ripe grapes among them. After finishing the painting, she told her to sell it at the market. This was done, and the skirt fetched enough money to buy a new one for the original owner and for the lady herself.

The use of coloring as the main method of drawing, as explained above, and the painting of ordinary objects, were the two distinctive features of Saimdang's style of painting. This style was a bold departure from the dominant tradition of calligraphic painting. As a woman in a highly stratified Confucian society, she could never attain the status of a professional artist. Unlike her male contemporaries, she could not move in the social circles of scholar-painters. However, these very obstacles invested her art with a distinctive originality.

Her work is much closer to folk tradition than it is to the calligraphic art of the literary tradition. At the same time, her paintings are imbued with a style and refinement not found in folk art. For this reason, dozens of poets and scholars during the Choson Dynasty wrote commentaries or forewords[19] to her paintings, and commissioned works by her hand. King Sukjong was struck with admiration when he saw a painting of Saimdang's at his father-in-law's house, and even ordered a replica to be made and kept in the palace, personally composing a foreword to it.

Saimdang established the painting of plants and insects as a distinguished genre in Korean art. Enriching the tradition of Korean painting, her contribution to the field was immeasurable.

---

[19] During the Choson Dynasty, it was customary for scholars and upper-class men to compose essays on art pieces such as paintings and calligraphy, as a way of showing their abilities in artistic appreciation and criticism.

Watermelons and Mice

Color on paper, 34cm x 28.3cm, National Museum of Korea

Eggplants and Bees

Color on paper, 34cm x 28.3cm, National Museum of Korea

Poppies and Lizard

Color on paper, 34cm x 28.3cm, National Museum of Korea

Cockscomb and Dung Beetles

Color on paper, 34cm x 28.3cm, National Museum of Korea

6. Remembering the Meaning of "Saimdang"

Saimdang was a dutiful daughter, an exemplary wife and a wise mother, in addition to being an eminent artist. She tried hard to express her individuality and achieve excellence in every aspect of her life. While fulfilling a teacher's role in relation to her husband, she raised her children to become renowned artists, government officials, philosophers, and scholars, while simultaneously attaining distinction for herself as an artist. It can be said that her accomplishments were made possible by a combination of her own talent and a nurturing family background. But exceptional talent and a good upbringing do not automatically lead to great moral and artistic accomplishments, unless they are accompanied by determination and self-discipline.

As a woman of intellect and perception, she could not have been unaware of the restrictions and limitations of the society in which she lived. Considering the firmly held tenet of female inferiority, and the oppressive customs to which women were subjected during the Choson Dynasty, it is hard to imagine that such remarkable accomplishments were possible without great inner strength and resolve. Through her life and her art, Saimdang demonstrated that such inner strength results in love and compassion for people and the world. Aside from her art, the greatest issue of her strength and compassion was her son, Yulgok, whose scholarship and devotion to the country were to have a lasting impact on the history of Korea.

References

Cho, Yongjin. *Shin Saimdang, a Painter Who Loved Plants and Insects*, Seoul: Namusup, 2005.

Shin, Hyesook. "A Study of Shin Saimdang," Master's Thesis, Sungshin Women's University, Department of Education, 1990.

Sohn, Insoo. *The Life and Lessons of Shin Saimdang*, Seoul: Bakyoungsa, 1976.

Yi, Eunsang. *Saimdang and Yulgok*, Seoul: Sungmungak, 1980.

_____. *The Life and Art of Saimdang*, Seoul: Sungmungak, 1994.

Yi, Yi. "A Record of Late Mother's Life," *A Collection of Yulgok's Writing*, Sungnam: Institute of Korean Studies, 1988a.

_____. "The Story of Maternal Grandmother Moving the Heaven," *A Collection of Yulgok's Writing*, Sungnam: Institute of Korean Studies. 1988b.

Yi Yulgok: His Life, Character, and Scholarship

In terms of their fundamental nature, the ordinary person and the great sage are not different. There are differences between people, because some have greater talent and are purer in heart than others. Yet if one sincerely tries to do away with old habits and recover one's true human nature, the result will be an infinite number of good deeds. Therefore, why should an ordinary person not aspire to be a sage?

– From *Kyok-mong-yo-gyol*[20] by Yi Yulgok

Yulgok Yi Yi[21] (1536~1584) was the most distinguished Confucian scholar of the Choson Dynasty (1392~1910), together with Toegye Yi Hwang (1501~1570). He was also a statesman and conscientious administrator. Yulgok has been compared to the eccentric peak of a summer time

---

[20] Yulgok wrote this book in 1577 to provide a basic study guideline for beginner scholars. After its composition, the book was widely used as a textbook in secondary schools until the end of the Choson Dynasty (1392~1910). The title of the book means "repelling ignorance."

[21] "Yulgok" is a courtesy name of Yi Yi, originating from the name of his ancestral place. "Yulgok," "Yi Yulgok" or "Yi Yi" are used to refer to him.

Portrait of Yi Yulgok

clouds, and Toegye to the warmth and splendor of the lakes in spring time. As a philosopher, he established a new paradigm of exemplary conduct, and as a statesman, he proposed deep and sweeping reforms. His conviction was that the purpose of learning was ultimately to apply what one had learned practically in real life, and his life and deeds answer to this conviction. He contemplated profound philosophical questions about human ethics and the purpose of the universe, but he did not stop at ideas. He pursued policy reforms with passion, with the aim of fully realizing the Confucian ideals in human society, and even dared to offer corrective advice to the King, in the face of a majority of statesmen in the court who opposed his views. He comprehended the international politics of the day, and foresaw the great misfortune that was heading towards his country. Even on his deathbed, he continued to exert himself for his King and his people. A Confucian to his very heart, he espoused a society founded on the Confucian social order, and yet he appreciated the dignity of the human being, which he believed was equal in all people regardless of social status. Hence, he was aptly compared to "the eccentric peak of a summer time cloud," in view of his remarkable character and prominence in his own day. Combined with the careful education he received from his mother Shin Saimdang, his scholastic endeavors and inner discipline made Yulgok one of the greatest and most significant figures in Korean history. Considering that his lifetime of 47 years was relatively short, his impression upon his country's culture and traditions was great and far-reaching.

1. A Black Dragon Swoops In

In the spring of the year in which Yulgok was born (1536), his mother Shin Saimdang had a mysterious dream. In the dream, Saimdang made a journey to the East Sea, and a sea nymph emerged from the waves with a baby boy in her arms. The skin of the baby boy shone and sparkled with an unnatural brightness. The sea nymph gave the baby to Saimdang, and she awoke. Soon after the dream, she began to show signs of pregnancy, and on the night before the baby was born, she had another auspicious dream. This time, a black dragon soared upwards out of the sea, flew to her bedroom and landed on the balcony. For this reason, Yulgok's boyhood name was "Hyunyong," literally meaning "a dragon manifests itself." His birth room was called Mongyongsil (lit. "Room of Dragon Dream"). When Yulgok grew to be 11 years old, his father, Yi Wonsu, also had an unusual dream. In the dream, a sage-like old man pointed to the boy Yulgok and said, "This child will be reckoned among the greatest philosophers of our land. Therefore, let his name be Yi." From then on, the letter "Yi" was used for his given name. The Chinese character of "Yi" refers to a halo, or corona, and was here used to signify the future greatness of Yulgok.

As these dreams portended, Yulgok showed an extraordinary precociousness from a very early age, and a strong sense of right and wrong. His biographies state that as soon as he learned to speak, he was able to read. There are several episodes that testify to his intellectual ability. At the age of three, his grandmother took up a pomegranate and asked him, "What is this like?" Yulgok replied with a phrase from an old poem, "Broken red gemstones are wrapped in the skin of a pomegranate," to the amusement and surprise of all. At the age of four, his teacher made an error in the interpretation of a sentence in a certain text. Yulgok looked quietly at the sentence in question, and then gave his own interpretation, which the teacher acknowledged to be correct.

Throughout his childhood, Yulgok was widely known as a prodigy. His intellectual progress was so fast that, at the age of 10, he had read all the major historical works, and the classics of Taoism and Confucianism. His progress received official recognition when he passed the qualification for the civil service examination at the age of only thirteen. At the time, there was another prodigy taking the exam, who was the same age as Yulgok. As both of them passed, the court officials in charge of the examination were very impressed, and arranged to meet with them. The other boy was apparently very boastful, while Yulgok was modest and humble. Many who witnessed this meeting foresaw that Yulgok would become a great scholar and a man of character. Later at the age of 29, Yulgok won first place at the final stage of the examination. The civil service examination consisted of many stages, and candidates had to pass through the beginner and intermediate stages before reaching the finals. Yulgok's achievements became legendary after he succeeded in securing first place in every one of the nine exams.

However, it was not just his intellectual acumen that distinguished Yulgok as extraordinary. The following episode, which occurred when he was five years old, shows his humanity and compassion. A man crossing a river slipped and fell into the water. Many people laughed at the frantic attempts of the poor man to climb out, but Yulgok, a child at the time, clung to a nearby pillar in great consternation at the man's plight. Only when the man reached safety did he finally relax. The warm heart and sense of justice that the young Yulgok had showed continued to characterize his life, bearing fruit in his service to the nation.

A poem, written at the age of 8, reveals Yulgok's genius in its verses. He wrote this poem while visiting a riverside pavilion at his family estate in Paju.

> Autumn is deep at a wooded pavilion,
> Wandering endlessly the poet's mind.
> Water flows far into the sky,
> Leaves mirror the red of the sun,
> Mountains reflect the lonely moon,

The river holds a thousand breaths of the wind.
Wild geese fly over and away,
Quiet among the clouds of echoes.

In this poem, the phrases about the moon and river are particularly striking. They appear to say that the moon rises high above all else, while the river flows calmly, taking in countless breaths of wind. The poem is a witness to Yulgok's aspiring spirit as well as his understanding of nature. At the same time, it also seems to foretell his short and difficult life as a progressive reformer, just as the sounds of wild geese are halted by the clouds.

2. Filial Devotion

Like his mother, Shin Saimdang, Yulgok was known for his filial devotion from early childhood. When Saimdang once fell seriously ill, Yulgok, then only 3 years old, went into the ancestral shrine to pray for his mother. At 9, when his father became ill and was in a coma, he cut his arm to let drops of blood fall into his father's mouth. He then prayed to the ancestors to take his life instead of his father's. At the age of 14, when Saimdang passed away, he and his brothers together held a three-year mourning period at the burial site. During this time, they dressed in full mourning attire, and personally carried out all the ceremonial procedures, from setting the daily memorial table to washing the dishes, and left none of the duties to the servants. After the customary mourning period, Yulgok continued to mourn in conscience for another year. "Mourning in conscience" means to continue to grieve in the ceremonial manner even though the official mourning period has ended. Although mourning at the burial site of one's parents was common among aristocrats at the day, Yulgok, who was only 14, practiced it out of a genuine affection and respect for his mother. The Choson Sillok (Annals of the Choson Dynasty) recorded, "Yi Yi held a funeral for his mother with sincere devotion." He paid further tribute to his mother by writing *A Record of My Late Mother's Life*, which remains an important historical source about Saimdang's life and art. Later Yulgok performed a mourning ceremony at the burial site of his father as well.

Yulgok was known for the love and filial devotion he had for his maternal grandmother as well. His grandmother had always shown a special concern for Yulgok, but his behavior in this regard was exceptional, considering that throughout the Choson Dynasty, the maternal line was regarded as less important than the paternal line. Yulgok, however, was born and lived at his grandparents' house until he reached the age of five. After Saimdang's death, his great affection for his grandmother would naturally have developed even further.

When he was 31 years old, he was appointed to the post of Civil Affairs official after returning from a diplomatic trip to China. Hearing that his 89 year old grandmother was seriously ill, he immediately resigned his post and left for his grandmother's house. This incident became a minor scandal in the court, since he had left before he was permitted to do so. Certain officials pressed strongly for his dismissal as punishment for his error. The King did not listen to them, however, reasoning that Yulgok's act signified great filial piety, rather than disloyalty to his country. Yulgok also wrote *An Account of the Virtuous Acts of Lady Yi* to record how his grandmother had come to be awarded a monument of virtue by the court. The story of her sacrificial prayer for her husband (Yulgok's grandfather) is narrated earlier in this book.

The stories we have regarding Yulgok's step-mother tell of his self-discipline as well as filial devotion. Shin Saimdang told her husband not to marry another woman if she should die early, as in fact she did. With regard to Saimdang's request, Yulgok's father entrusted the management of his household to a concubine, instead of formally marrying someone of his own class. The concubine was a commoner by birth, rude and coarse in her manner. She did not treat Yulgok and his siblings well, and when Yulgok, at the age of 17, entered the temple at Mt. Kumgang for a year to practice Buddhism, some supposed that the real reason he had left was to escape from his step-mother.

When Yulgok's father passed away, his step-mother began to drink *soju* (rice wine) in the morning, a habit formed out of loneliness. Instead of criticizing her, Yulgok called on her every morning, and warmed a wine jar himself before serving her. He took good care of his step-mother so that she would not feel isolated from the rest of the family members. His step-mother's attitude towards him eventually softened, and later when Yulgok passed away, she remained in mourning for three years in expression of her deep gratitude.

3. Scholarship

Yulgok was a gentleman scholar, an archetype of the ruling class of the Choson Dynasty (1392~1910). Although the aristocracy of Choson consisted of two categories – scholars and warriors – greater honor was generally conferred on the former. Within the Confucian tradition, scholarship was regarded as the true occupation of the aristocratic man. The sway of Confucianism was absolute during the Choson Dynasty, as the nation had been re-established on the Neo-Confucian system of rule and governance. With the beginning of the new dynasty, Confucianism had become the state religion and basis of government.

Neo-Confucianism was a synthesis of classical Confucianism and other philosophical traditions such as Buddhism and Taoism. This new school of thought had been developed by Chu Hsi and the brothers Cheng during the Sung dynasty (960~1270) of China. The founders of Choson envisioned their new nation to be the realization of the Neo-Confucian paradigm. Therefore, while Buddhism was the national religion during the Koryo Dynasty,[22] Choson made a policy of repressing Buddhism, as well as Taoism and even other currents of Confucianism, and the ruling class in particular shunned their study and practice.

Yulgok, however, was an original thinker. He critically assessed the dominant Cheng-Chu school of Confucianism and freely drew on the insights of other traditions to develop his own ideas. In his poems, he makes frequent

---

[22] The Koryo dynasty lasted from A. D. 918 to 1392.

reference Lao-tzu and Chang-tzu, the founders of Taoism. He even wrote a commentary on *Tao-Te Ching* by the former.[23] Moreover, after his mother passed away, Yulgok went to Mt. Kumgang to learn from the monks about the Buddhist scriptures, and practiced Buddhist meditation. His understanding of Buddhist concepts and his practice of Buddhist meditation surprised many of the monks he met. He eventually left Mt. Kumgang, having reached the conclusion that the Buddhist notion "Mind is Buddha" was no different from the central Confucian concept of "true human nature." Even though it was only for one year at a young age, the episode is a clear sign of his non-conformist approach. Thanks to his open-mindedness in learning, Yulgok could carve his own philosophical perspective out of the existing Confucian tradition.

4. Self-Discipline

To Confucian scholars, the most important virtue was to put one's knowledge into practice. "To learn, and then to act" was a Confucian tenet that required inner discipline. In this regard, Yulgok was genuinely an exemplary figure, and tried hard to live up to the ideal throughout his life. His resolution is clearly seen in two pieces of his writing in particular. One is

---

[23] Hwang, Jun-Yeon (1995), *An Understanding of Yulgok's Philosophy*, Seoul: Seo gwangsa. P. 55. *Tao-Te Ching* is translated as *The Book of the Way and Its Virtu e*. Written in 600 B. C. by Lao-tzu, it is a classical text fundamental to the Taoi st school of Chinese philosophy.

"Minding The Self", written after he returned from Mt. Kumgang at the age of 18. It tells of his resolve to follow the example of the sages and other great men, how to conduct everyday speech and behavior, and the correct attitude to learning. In it he says, "Learning should be neither hurried nor desultory. It should cease only at death. If one seeks to reap the rewards of learning too soon, this is greed. If one does not pursue learning, this is a disgrace, and one is no longer human." Here "learning" means more than academic study. More precisely, it means disciplining and cultivating one's mind according to the principles of the heavens.

Another work which deals with self-discipline is "Repentance On Winter Solstice." Yulgok wrote it at midnight on the winter solstice, in a reflection on his life up to that day, at the age of 23 years old. Contemplating the many changes in the world and the universe, he came to realize: "When all is in flux, is it not right that I too should change?" The following poem goes into detail about aspects of himself he wishes to change:

> The cycle of the Heaven is about to repeat itself,
> Filling me with awe and wonder.
> The cosmic essence lives and breathes in all things,
> The three elements of Heaven, Earth, and Man.
> Virtue is the gift of Heaven,
> As bright as the moon and the sun.
> But foolish thoughts have dimmed its brightness,
> Small at first, but great in time.
> As an ax devours the tree,

Foolishness has gnawed at my soul.
These five and twenty years[24]
I have been lost in a deep slumber.
Looking back on the wrongs of yesterday,
My mind is filled with shock and sorrow.
Now, with all my heart and mind,
I vow to be awakened.
Heavens, may you see and hear.

Yulgok put reverence at the center of his life, and regarded learning to practice reverence as the ultimate purpose of academic study. He warned himself against mere bookishness and sought to apply knowledge and moral lessons in real life.

An episode from his forty-fifth year illustrates his inner discipline. Yulgok was at the time making frequent diplomatic missions to a northern town called Hwangju. In this town, there was a *kisaeng* (professional female entertainer), named Yuji. Yuji had known Yulgok since she was an apprentice *kisaeng*. Now a grown woman, she had fallen in love with him.

One night, Yuji appeared outside Yulgok's residence. Yulgok said, "If I close the door, I close my heart. But if I share her bed, I harm my soul." He thus allowed her to come in, but showed her to a separate bedroom. Thinking that rejecting her outright would be uncompassionate, but spending the night

---

[24] At the time, Yulgok was 23 years old in the Western terms. But he was 25 years old according to the Korean way of counting, according to which one is 1 year old at the moment of birth and a year is added every New Year's Day (not at one's birthday). Except in direct quotations, the Western way of counting is used in this essay.

with her out of desire would be unjust, he found a middle ground. Yulgok was candid and frank enough to write a poem in praise of the beauty of Yuji, but he did not lose his presence of mind or self-control. Later when Yulgok passed away, Yuji mourned him for three years, as if he were a family member.

Yulgok lived a life of integrity and honesty. When he came into possession of a house, he immediately sold it and shared the money amongst his poorest relatives. At times he barely had enough to feed himself. A statesman recorded, "When Yulgok passed away, his family was so poor that they had to borrow clothes to dress the body. Not having a house of their own in Seoul, they were constantly on the move, suffering from cold and hunger. Yulgok's friends and the other scholars all contributed to buy them a house." At the time, it was common for government officials to embezzle funds and abuse their position. But Yulgok was exemplary and heroic in his inner discipline and dedication to the country's good.

5. Visiting Toegye

Yulgok visited the great scholar, Toegye, when he was 21 years old and when Toegye was 57. Although Yulgok had won the first place at the civil service examination a year before, he was still largely unknown. By contrast, Toegye had long been renowned for his scholarship and virtuous conduct. However, when they met each other, Toegye recognized Yulgok's character and potential. In a letter to one of his students, Toegye wrote: "He [Yulgok] is positive and cheerful in personality, and has a brilliant memory. He is thoroughly set upon learning. A sage once said, 'A man must respect his juniors.' I now appreciate the wisdom of this saying." Of Yulgok's poems, he wrote, "The poems are worth reading, though not as good as the man himself." By this, Toegye meant Yulgok's poems did not fully represent his noble character. Toegye acknowledged Yulgok's genius and greatly encouraged his aspirations. Later in a letter to Yulgok, he wrote, "In these present days, when other men greedily pursue their own interests, I am very thankful that you at least are trying to find a way to the greatest virtue." Toegye correctly foresaw that Yulgok would become an important person.

For his part, Yulgok appreciated Toegye's depth of thought and moral probity, and regarded him as a mentor. He wrote many letters to Toegye to ask his opinion on matters of philosophy and other subjects, and to articulate his own ideas. Twelve years later when Toegye passed away, he composed a funeral oration. To show his respect for his mentor, he wore a white robe and mourned for him in conscience.

Toegye, or Yi Hwang, was a scholar who opened up new possibilities contained within the Neo-Confucian philosophy. He fashioned a creative synthesis based on a comprehensive survey of past works by Chinese and Korean scholars. Yulgok was able to elaborate his own philosophical framework using the foundation Toegye had laid.[25] In the letters that the two scholars exchanged, differences of opinion are very infrequent. But in the last

---

[25] Yi, Jong-Ho (1994), *Yulgok: His Character and Ideas*, Seoul: Jisik, p. 57.

letter that Yulgok sent to Toegye in his mid-thirties, we see evidence that he was growing more critical of Toegye's theories. Yulgok's fully matured philosophy differs from Toegye's in several important respects. Eventually, Toegye and Yulgok came to represent two distinct schools of Korean Neo-Confucian philosophy, that is, the *Yongnam* school and *Kiho* school respectively.

6. Contemplating the Nature of the Mind

In spite of an unstable economy and a volatile political situation, the period of the Choson Dynasty in which Yulgok lived was a time of great progress in the fields of literature and philosophy. Thanks to the Choson scholars who had expanded the theories of Neo-Confucianism and developed them to a further level of sophistication, the new philosophy had become firmly established.

The "School of Human Nature and Principle"[26] served as the orthodox school of Neo-Confucianism in Choson. Also known as the Cheng-Chu school or Chu-Hsi school, it is associated with Song Chinese thinkers such as Cheng I (1033~1107) and Chu Hsi (1130~1200). While classical Confucianism, as taught by Confucius and Mencius, remained focused on the morality and ethics of the human society, the Cheng-Chu school of Neo-Confucianism grew to encompass metaphysics and psychology. From this

---

[26] *Sung-li-hak* (Korean), *Hsing-li-hsueh* (Chinese)

was derived the name *Sung-li-hak*, or the "School of Human Nature (*sung*) and Principle (*li*)."

The main concepts of the school were as follows. *Li* means principle, reason, truth, law or pattern. It refers to the underlying laws of the cosmos and of nature. The *li* of human nature specifically is called *sung*. *Ki* (*Chi* in Chinese) refers to material force or energy. Due to the workings of *ki*, cosmic transformations are possible, and through it everything comes to exist. *Li* is the principle behind every phenomenon, and *ki* is the material cause behind it. *Li* and *ki* together make up s*im* (mind). *Jung* (emotion) arises when the mind responds to the outside world.

Yulgok's contribution to the development of the Neo-Confucian philosophy centers around two metaphysical issues. One was the issue of human emotion in relation to *li* and *ki*, which eventually came to be called the "Four-Seven debate." The other was the question as to whether the nature of humans was the same as that of other beings, such as animals. The Four-Seven debate initially began between Toegye and Kobong, another philosopher. Yulgok re-opened the debate thirteen years later. By further elaborating on the issues explored by his two predecessors, he resolved some of the disputed points and built a unique and compelling frame of metaphysics with profound philosophical, ethical, and political ramifications.

The Four-Seven debate marks one of the most important events in Korean philosophical development. It culminated in a distinctively Korean interpretation of Neo-Confucianism, and is testament to the vitality and maturity of the intellectual world in sixteenth century Korea. The debate reached its height at the time of Toegye and Yulgok, and lasted for three more centuries, engendering fierce controversy among Choson scholars.[27]

"Four-Seven" refers to the "four beginnings of virtue" and "seven emotions." According to Mencius and Chu Hsi, the principles of human nature are the virtues of benevolence, righteousness, propriety, and wisdom. The virtue of benevolence is manifested in the ability to empathize with another; righteousness in the ability to feel shame and aversion; propriety in the inclination towards courtesy and modesty; and wisdom in the understanding of right and wrong. These four feelings come from the original essence of human nature, and therefore are called the Four Beginnings. The seven emotions refer to joy, anger, sorrow, fear, love, hatred, and desire, and constitute the totality of a human feeling.

Although the Four Beginnings and the Seven Emotions were important concepts in Neo-Confucianism, the link between them was not clearly articulated by Chinese thinkers. Choson scholars undertook the task of understanding the relationship between the "Four" and the "Seven," and ultimately between *li* and *ki*. Toegye asserted that the Four Beginnings should be understood in terms of *li* and the Seven Emotions in terms of *ki*, making a clear distinction between the manifestation of *li* and the manifestation of *ki*. For him, the Four Beginnings are the manifestation of the cosmic principle (*li*), whereas the Seven Emotions are aroused by physical and material conditions, and thus the manifestation of *ki*. His position was that *li* and *ki* are

---

[27] Chung, Edward Y. J. (1995), *The Korean Neo-Confucianism of Yi T'oegye and Yi Yulgok*, Albany, NY: SUNY Press, p. xiv.

independent from each other and become two different sources of human feelings. Kobong challenged Toegye's view, by arguing that *li* cannot exist apart from *ki*. He maintained that *li* and *ki* are inseparable in regard to concrete phenomena including the mind and feelings.[28]

When Yulgok took up the issue years later, he adopted Kobong's position and developed it into a clearer, more original and systematic viewpoint. While Kobong somewhat modified his initial position after the debates with Toegye, Yulgok totally opposed Toegye's dualistic thesis. He criticized Toegye for postulating two different sources of goodness. According to Yulgok, because *li* and *ki* are always inseparable in physical phenomena, it is not possible to have one group of feelings (the Four) as manifestations of *li* and the other group of feelings (the Seven) as manifestations of *ki*. From Yulgok's point of view, the Four are rooted within the Seven as a subset consisting of "good" feelings. Thus the Four encompasses good only, while the Seven includes both good and evil.[29]

Toegye, as a dualistic thinker, separated the mind into two parts: the moral mind and the human mind, assigning the Four to the former, and the Seven to the latter. By contrast, Yulgok argued that the mind is fundamentally one and cannot be separated into two minds. This is because the Seven, or the totality of feelings, include both the moral mind and the human mind together. Yulgok stressed that the moral mind and the human mind refer simply to two dimensions of one mind—virtuous and emotional. Unlike Toegye, Yulgok

---

[28] Chung (1995), pp. 48-58.
[29] Chung (1995), p. 168.

strenuously asserted the inseparability of *li* and *ki* in the phenomenal world. While Toegye assigned an active role to *li* so that it could manifest itself in human feelings, Yulgok insisted whereas *ki* can operate as an active force, *li* cannot. Therefore *li* exists within *ki*, but cannot exist outside *ki*.[30']

Yulgok went further to present an original hypothesis about the interdependent relationship of *li* and *ki*. In his expression, "*Li* encompasses, while *ki* is limited."

> Why is it said that "*li* encompasses?" *Li* has neither a beginning nor an end, neither before nor after...For this reason, as *li* rides on the circulating movement of *ki*, it creates irregularities and non-uniformities. Its original mystery, however, exists everywhere. Where *ki* is partial, *li* is also partial. But in this case, what is partial is *ki*, not *li*. Equally, where *ki* is complete, what is complete is *ki*, not *li*. *Li* exists everywhere, even in ashes, dregs, excrement, soil, and dirt, each of which has its own nature. Still, the original subtlety of *li* is not diminished. This is what I mean when I say that "*li* encompasses." Why is it said, "*Ki* is limited?" *Ki* already incorporates physical form and traces of the material; therefore, it has a beginning and end, before and after...Since *ki* moves without ceasing, ascending and descending, flitting and fleeting, it is irregular and uneven, and thus gives rise to myriad changes...This is what I mean by saying that "*ki* is limited."[31]

---

[30] Chung (1995), pp. 163-175.
[31] Translation from Chung (1995), pp. 114-115.

Yulgok applied the above theory to address the issue of whether humans and animals have the same nature. He concluded that humans and animals are not the same, because of the discriminative force of *ki*. Humans and animals are the same in principle, because of the universality of encompassing *li*.[32] After Yulgok, in the seventeenth century, philosophical explorations of this issue advanced further. In Yulgok's theory of the inseparability and interdependence of *li* and *ki*, we can detect traces of Taoist and Buddhist influence, which appear to have influenced his appraisal of the orthodox Cheng-Chu school of Neo-Confucianism.[33]

This metaphysical thesis of *li* and *ki* had ethical, educational, and political implications. Yulgok presented a very optimistic viewpoint, namely that basic human desires are part of human nature and can be transformed into positive impulses. In his view, the sages and ordinary people are born equal, in the sense that they all have fundamental instincts and desires. The one crucial difference in the case of the sage is that the human mind follows and is subject to the moral mind. The conclusion is therefore that even though one may begin with a human mind caught up in basic feelings and desires, one can always give sovereignty to the moral mind if one follows moral principles and overcomes selfish desires.[34]

Yulgok's philosophical stance was directly related to his deep sense of social and political responsibility. Yulgok took government administration very seriously and believed it was an important part of his duty as a

---

[32] Hwang (1995), pp. 97-103.
[33] Chung (1995), pp. 115-116; Hwang (1995), p. 96.
[34] Chung (1995), pp. 94-96.

practitioner of Confucianism, working as an official and statesman almost continuously, following his first appointment at the age of 27. This contrasts with Toegye, who spent most of his adult years in study and self-cultivation, and held an official position in the court only briefly. It can be said that while Toegye tended towards abstract idealism, Yulgok was a pragmatic reformer. His reform efforts will be covered in greater detail shortly.

Yulgok wrote many books, philosophical treatises, political memorials, and letters. Most of these were published in *Complete Works of Yi Yulgok* (1611). Among them, the *Outline of the Learning of Sagehood* (*Sung-hak-sip-yo*), his most famous philosophical work, contains the fundamentals of Confucian metaphysics, ethics, self-cultivation, and statecraft.[35] Written a few years after his work on the "Four-Seven" debate, it sets forth the essence of Yulgok's philosophy in its maturity, and paints a vivid picture of Choson's intellectual world. Later King Youngjo wrote a preface to the book and vowed to put its teachings into practice. Yulgok's political memorials include *Ten Thousand Character Memorial* (*Man-un-bong-sa*) and *Dongho Questions and Answers* (*Dong-ho-mun-dap*), the latter of which consists of eleven articles on political reform. Yulgok wrote books on education as well. *Model for an Academy* (*Hak-gyo-mo-bum*) is an educational treatise on the goals and methods of youth education, while *Essential Instructions of Kyukmong* (*Kyuk-mong-yo-gyul*) is a systematic study guide for beginner students. His commitment to education was such that, at the age of 41, he opened a school called *Eun-byung-jung-sa* in Haeju and taught many young scholars there.

---

[35] Chung (1995), p. 31.

Later *Eun-byung-jung-sa* became a center for his followers and students.

7.   The Reformist Vision

Starting his public career at the age of 27, Yulgok worked as a government official and statesman for about twenty years until he died at the age of 47. In his career, he vigorously pursued reforms in many areas, particularly regarding domestic issues and national defense. Taxation, military conscription, and the civil service examination, were all targeted with bold reforms that required changes to be made to the existing class system, benefiting the commoners and other disadvantaged people. As his reformist vision was against the interests of those in power, he faced resistance, opposition, and even the threat of dismissal, whenever he proposed such reforms. Nevertheless, he was tireless in his efforts.

Much of the mid-Choson period was spent in political turmoil, so that many conscientious scholars, including Yulgok's maternal grandfather, purposely decided not to pursue a public career. Domestic politics had become more secure by the time Yulgok came of age, but it was far from being totally safe. Furthermore, the country's economy was in a precarious position, and the people's daily lives were greatly burdened. Outside Korea, the Qing family were about to overthrow the Ming dynasty in China, while in Japan, Hideyosi Toyotomi, later responsible for the Japanese invasion of Korea in 1592, was rising to power. Yulgok understood what this portended and what needed to be done, more clearly than any other statesmen at the time.

Yulgok believed strongly that the nation needed to transform itself in order to survive. He warned that the ruling establishment was like a sick old man, and would fall unless it underwent a thorough and far-reaching process of reform.[36] In a letter to Toegye, written when he was 30 years old, he voiced his concerns as follows: "It has been some 20 years since this country sank into these ongoing troubles, but since all the statesmen and officials on every level are wedded to convention, they are unable to improve the situation even slightly. It is unclear how much longer the people will endure, and our national finances are exhausted. Without reform, the country will, I am afraid, not remain a nation. As for me, a government official, am I any different from a swallow that has built its nest on a billowing unmoored tent? Thinking about the current state of our nation, I am kept awake throughout the night."

Perceiving reform as a matter of national destiny, Yulgok proposed radical measures, in particular pertaining to freedom of speech, self-regulation of the governing sectors, and effective personnel management. A firmly-held belief of Yulgok was that knowledge of public opinion was a foundation of good governance. He advised the King that freedom of speech must be encouraged, so that the ruler would know clearly what his people wanted. Second, Yulgok urged that in order to restore the integrity of the government, bribery had to be eliminated altogether. At the time, corrupt practices were commonplace

---

[36] Hwang (1995), pp. 224-240.

among government officials of every rank. Third, Yulgok recommended that those born of concubines should be allowed to qualify to take the civil service examination. In Choson, concubines were legally permitted to the ruling class, but children from such unions were not given the same status as the father. Because only men of aristocratic status were qualified to take civil service examination, they had no prospects of a public career and thus inhabited a social limbo. Yulgok reasoned that only the talent and character of a person should be taken into account, and not his background. Moreover, he also proposed to lessen the compulsory duties of servants belonging to government offices, and is recorded as saying "Servants also rank among our people." It is true that his reform measures fall short of modern democracy. Nonetheless, it would be fair to say that Yulgok strived to establish a more egalitarian and democratic society in the context of the highly stratified Neo-Confucian social order.[37]

Yulgok continually advised the King to test new reforms in order to make the nation more stable and prosperous. But the King and most other statesmen did not understand the urgency of change, and thus their actions were of little use. Rather, many of them considered that Yulgok's proposals were unbalanced, and that he was even exaggerating some of society's problems. In this political climate, his ideas for reform could not be realized. At the time, the Choson Dynasty was in great need of visionaries like Yulgok, but the royal court and the ruling class were not ready either to implement or to accept any of his plans.

---

[37] Chung (1995), p. 160.

8.   Proposal to Train One Hundred Thousand Soldiers

Yulgok was appointed Minister of Defense in 1582, when he was 45 years old. In February of the next year, he presented a political treatise to the King, entitled "Six Urgent Programs for the State." The six programs were as follows: first, to appoint wise and capable persons to government positions; second, to train soldiers; third, to replenish state funds; fourth, to guard the border securely; fifth, to prepare cavalry horses; sixth, to educate the people.

In March, he made a proposal to spend "ten years saving, ten years educating, and ten years training military forces." Finally in April, his proposal developed into one of training 100,000 soldiers for national defense. In his own words addressed to the King: "We must train one hundred thousand soldiers in order to prepare our nation for a military emergency. Otherwise, within the next ten years, there will be a disaster, just as when a dirt wall collapses all at once. Let Your Highness gather and train one hundred thousand soldiers. Twenty thousand of these should be placed in Seoul, and ten thousand in each of the eight prefectures. The soldiers should be exempt from other duties and given military training. In time of peace, let them take turns to guard the capital, but in time of war, let them come together for our national defense. If we do not prepare in advance, we will be unable to do anything should an emergency arise, and have no choice but to drive untrained people into the fields of war. Then we will be without hope."

The proposal to train 100,000 soldiers came out of an acute sense of crisis on Yulgok's part. He had been following the international developments around the Korean peninsula carefully, and was concerned that the country was unstable domestically and highly vulnerable to its neighbors. King Seonjo seemed initially inclined to favor Yulgok's proposals, but a prominent statesman by the name of Yu Songnyong set up a vigorous opposition to the plan. Yu reasoned that training military forces in time of peace would serve only to provoke neighboring countries, and his point of view gained the support of other officials. In June, Yulgok was impeached by a group of fellow statesmen on the charge of "abusing his power and humiliating the king." The purpose of this group was to put pressure on the King to dismiss Yulgok from office. Yulgok himself offered to resign six times, and was each time refused by the King. King Seonjo trusted Yulgok greatly, but owing to mounting pressure eventually had to accept his withdrawal from the government. Both the King and his advisers would live to regret their decision, and had ample time to contemplate their foolishness during the disastrous events that followed.

Yulgok passed away in the January of the following year. Within less than a decade, the country was invaded by Japan. Just as he had feared, Choson was thoroughly unprepared to defend itself. Yu, who had thwarted Yulgok's proposal, shed tears of contrition and declared, "Yulgok was truly a leader, thinker, and sage." He realized with sorrow that Yulgok's advice had been inspired by his deep sense of responsibility for the country and people, as well as his grasp of reality.

9.   A Black Dragon Flies Away

While other government ministers believed that they were enjoying the blessings of peace, Yulgok made an unblinkered appraisal of the geopolitics of the day, and proposed a practical solution to save the country. He lamented: "Alas! Our troubles in this country have never been more severe than now, and burdens of the people have never been heavier…The Book of Odes says, 'A boat on the river drifts with no destination. A mind that is disquieted has no resting place.' Even so is my troubled mind."

Yulgok's health was poor towards the end of his life, but following his effective dismissal from government, he became seriously ill and passed away soon afterwards. Two months before his death, the King re-appointed Yulgok as minister of internal affairs, hoping to implement the reform measures he had proposed. Unfortunately, it was too late.

Yulgok spent the final 13 days of his life confined to his bed. During these final days, he made no mention of family matters, but spoke only of national affairs. The day before his death, King Seonjo sent an official responsible for policing the border to Yulgok to ask his opinion. Family members and others advised him against meeting with the official. "My body exists only to serve the country," he replied, "Even if my illness worsens, this is my destiny." With help he raised himself into a sitting position, and his brother Wu took down his words as he dictated. This was to be his final work, "Six Articles for Guarding the Border."

When he had finished dictating, he collapsed and fell unconscious, as the exertion had drained him of energy. The final moment came later after an attack of asthma. He said, "Let me cut my nails and bathe." Lying down restfully after this, he died peacefully with his head directed eastwards. It was January 16th in 1584, the 17th year of the King Seonjo's reign, and he was 47 years old.

When the news of Yulgok's death came, King Seonjo wept. He ordered that no meat should be served at his meals, and cancelled three consecutive daily meetings of the cabinet. A scholar named Wu Seongjeon recorded: "Even country folk from remote villages cried and wailed in grief. University[38] students, soldiers, shopkeepers in the market place, lower officials in government offices, and people from all walks of life hurried to bow in front of the funeral altar, many of them shedding tears. When the funeral procession left Yulgok's home, the streets were filled with people bidding him farewell."

For a long time, Yulgok remained a cherished memory in the hearts of the common people and received tributes after his death. People in Haeju, where Yulgok had made a residence and opened a school, abstained from eating meat or holding wedding feasts on the anniversary of his passing. From the king down to the commoners, people respected him deeply for his devotion and compassion.

The night before his death, his wife the Lady Roh had a dream about a black dragon soaring out of the bedroom into the heavens. She remembered

---

[38] Choson had a national university called Sunggyungwan, with the aim of promoting Confucian scholarship.

that Yulgok's mother, Shin Saimdang, had dreamed of a black dragon flying towards her bedroom before she gave birth, and marveled that both the opening and closing of his life were marked by the same auspicious symbol, which signified a man of greatness.

The following story has been passed down concerning the foresight of Yi Yulgok. As stated, Yulgok perceived that a great disaster would follow from failures in national defense. His concerns became a catastrophic reality eight years after he had died, when Japan invaded Choson in 1592. The ensuing war lasted for seven years. During that time, tens of thousands of Koreans were killed, palaces, temples, and schools were burned down, national treasures were stolen, and many famous artisans were kidnapped and taken to Japan. Japanese soldiers would even cut the noses from the dead bodies and take them home as trophies of their victory. The nation of Choson was devastated to its very foundations.

As the war continued to go badly, King Seonjo was at one point forced to flee his palace in the capital and seek refuge in a remote part of the country. According to the story, the King and his retinue arrived at the banks of the Imjin River, north of Seoul, long after sunset. It was extremely dark and raining heavily. The King's attendants were at a loss as to how to cross the river in the dead of night, when they chanced upon a small pavilion near a ferry. They set this pavilion on fire to provide a light by which to work, and were able to convey the King safely across the river.

This pavilion had been built by one of Yulgok's ancestors. Yulgok had visited it frequently during his lifetime, with his mother and siblings when young, with friends and students when grown, and occasionally by himself. In later years when Yulgok was visiting the pavilion, he would make sure that his disciples carried a bottle of oil with them, and ordered them to apply the oil to the wooden floor. He would also apply pine resin to the pavilion pillars, and when asked why, he would reply that he was preparing for an emergency. Thanks to these measures, the pavilion could be used as a torch, and its flames were not extinguished even in the pouring rain.

Yulgok himself was a torch that shone brightly in the darkness of the age in which he lived. It is tragic indeed that his contemporaries chose not to see the reality which he might have shown them.

10. Yulgok, Still Living

Above all else, Yulgok was a man of action and of integrity. He is the most outstanding among the many prominent scholars of Choson Dynasty Korea, thanks to his tireless efforts to realize the Confucian ideals in the real world. While the Neo-Confucian scholarship of Choson has often been criticized by many later scholars for being overly theoretical, Yulgok was exceptional and even pioneering in his pragmatic reform efforts. He was a genuine "seonbi"[39] who sought to reach sagehood through self-cultivation on the one hand, and to improve the living conditions of ordinary people through

---

[39] "Seonbi" refers to an aristocratic scholar. In terms of social significance, "seon bi" is a counterpart to the "samurai" of Japan. The difference is that seonbi is a scholar, whereas samurai is a warrior.

Depictions of Shin Saimdang and Yi Yulgok on Korean Bank Notes[40]

action on the other. For his knowledge, filial devotion, compassion, and loyalty, he has been held up by subsequent generations as a model for study and imitation. As in his lifetime, he is still the most popular of all Confucian scholars amongst ordinary Koreans.

In its history, Korea has experienced many difficulties, owing in part to its geographic position between Japan and China. Yet, despite these difficulties, Koreans have maintained their identity as a nation. Yulgok is one of the national heroes that Koreans have traditionally looked up to as a representative of this identity, and is still alive in the hearts of his people today.

---

[40] The 5,000 won bill has a portrait of Yulgok, as well as pictures of his birthplace and Sin Saimdang's art. Sin Saimdang appears on the 50,000 bill.

References

Sources in Korean

Hwang, Jun-Yeon. *An Understanding of Yulgok's Philosophy*. Seoul: Seogwangsa, 1995.

_____. *Yi Yulgok: A Portrait of A Life*. Seoul: Seoul National University Press, 2000.

Yi, Eun-Sang. *Saimdang and Yulgok*. Seoul: Seongmungak, 1980.

Yi, Jong-Ho. *Yulgok: His Character and Ideas*. Seoul: Jisik, 1994.

Yi, Yi. *Kyuk-mong-yo-gyul*. Annotated by Hu-Soo Jung. Seoul: Jangnak, 2004 [1577].

Sources in English

Chung, Edward Y. J. *The Korean Neo-Confucianism of Yi T'oegye and Yi Yulgok*. Albany, NY: SUNY Press, 1995.

Authors

Hyang-Jin Jung is an associate professor in the department of anthropology at Seoul National University. Her research interests include self, emotion, education, American culture, and North Korea. She is currently conducting research about the emotional culture of the postmodern American society and cultural psychology of North Korea. She is the author of *Learning to Be an Individual: Emotion and Person in an American Junior High School* (Peter Lang, 2007).

Jiseon Lee is a full-time editor of the Korean Spirit and Culture series. She graduated in English Language and Literature from Ewha Womans University, and studied Literature and Philosophy at Wilson College and Boston College in the United States.

Editors

Hang-Jin Chang is a lawyer at Linklaters LLP in London, specializing in international finance. He read Law at Oxford University, and has extensive experience in Korean-English translations.

Yoon-Sang Han is a lawyer in New York City. He majored in Economics at Wesleyan University and received his law degree from William and Mary School of Law. He has translated various texts from Korean to English, including *Polishing the Diamond, Enlightening the Mind* (Wisdom Publications, 1999).

Matthew Jackson is a management consultant in London. He read Classics at Oxford University, and has worked for many years as an editor of English translations. He regularly writes on Korean issues, in particular the traditional arts and science.

Korean Spirit and Culture Website

www.kscpp.net

All booklets published in the series are available on our website, as well as additional materials covering various aspects of Korean history and culture.

Published so far:

Admiral Yi Sun-sin

King Sejong the Great

Chung Hyo Ye

Fifty Wonders of Korea

Master Wonhyo

The Practice of Hongik Ingan

Taste of Korea

Online video library includes:

Hangul, Alphabet of Compassion

UNESCO World Heritage in Korea

Korea Today: IT, Shipbuilding, Construction, Steel, Energy

And more…